THE
CASE FOR
REINCARNATION

About the Author

A native of Minnesota but a resident of Colorado since 1969, J. Allan Danelek's life has been a journey that has taken him down many different paths. Besides writing, his hobbies include art, political and military history, religion and spirituality, numismatics (coin collecting), paleontology, astronomy (and science in general), and Fortean subjects such as Bigfoot, UFOs, and things that go bump in the night. His personal philosophy is that life is about learning and growing, both intellectually and spiritually, and that is the perspective with which he approaches each project he undertakes. Jeff lives near Denver with his wife, Carol, and their two sons.

THE
CASE FOR
REINCARNATION

UNRAVELING
THE MYSTERIES OF
THE SOUL

J. ALLAN DANELEK

Llewellyn Publications
Woodbury, Minnesota

First Edition
First Printing, 2010

Cover art © Grant Faint/Photographer's Choice/PunchStock
Cover design by Ellen Dahl
Llewellyn is a registered trademark of Llewellyn Worldwide Ltd.

Library of Congress Cataloging-in-Publication Data
Danelek, J. Allan, 1958–
  The case for reincarnation : unraveling the mysteries of the soul /
J. Allan Danelek. — 1st ed.
    p. cm.
  Includes bibliographical references and index.
  ISBN 978-0-7387-1999-3
  1. Reincarnation. I. Title.
  BL515.D25 1010
  133.901'35—dc22
                          2009051925

Some passages in this book originally appeared in, or are adapted from, *Mystery of Reincarnation: The Evidence & Analysis of Rebirth*, also by J. Allan Danelek, and published in 2005 by Llewellyn Publications.

Llewellyn Worldwide Ltd. does not participate in, endorse, or have any authority or responsibility concerning private business transactions between our authors and the public.
  All mail addressed to the author is forwarded but the publisher cannot, unless specifically instructed by the author, give out an address or phone number.
  Any Internet references contained in this work are current at publication time, but the publisher cannot guarantee that a specific location will continue to be maintained. Please refer to the publisher's website for links to authors' websites and other sources.

Llewellyn Publications
Llewellyn Worldwide Ltd.
2143 Wooddale Drive
Woodbury, MN 55125-2989
www.llewellyn.com

Printed in the United States of America

Other Books by J. Allan Danelek

The Case for Ghosts: An Objective Look at the Paranormal

Mystery of Reincarnation: The Evidence & Analysis of Rebirth

Atlantis: Lessons from the Lost Continent

UFOs: The Great Debate: An Objective Look at Extraterrestrials, Government Cover-Ups, and the Prospect of First Contact

2012: Extinction or Utopia: Doomsday Prophecies Explored

Acknowledgments

It is said that nothing of importance is ever accomplished without the help of friends, and that is as true of writing a book as it is of shoveling a sidewalk. As such, I would be remiss not to acknowledge those who have been "in the loop" in putting this manuscript together, both for their willingness to read through the earliest drafts—when a work is still encased within its primordial goo—and for their willingness to make helpful suggestions. I'd especially like to thank Jim Schwartz for his invaluable assistance in explaining the process of hypnotism and past-life regression to me, as well as for sharing his personal opinions and anecdotes about some of the theories articulated in this book with regard to how they play out in his own work as a hypnotherapist. A special note of appreciation also goes to my sister, Cheri, for permitting me the rare opportunity of witnessing a past-life regression firsthand, and for allowing me to be a part of both her past and her present. And, finally, my wife, Carol, deserves special thanks for holding down the fort while I spent many an hour laboring away at the library. She is a young soul who travels well, and she fills my life with love and laughter. Thanks to all.

Contents

Preface

The reader may be aware that this is my second book on reincarnation[1] and may be wondering why I need to revisit the issue. The answer is simple: my first book was largely a treatment of the evidence for and against the teachings I gleaned from my studies in the subject over the years, with a small section that described the mechanism of how it worked from a layperson's perspective. Since then I've come to understand that most of my readers, already inclined to accept the belief beforehand, wanted to know more about how it all works—the "mechanics" of the process, so to speak. This book, then, is essentially a greatly expanded version of the second half of that earlier book, designed to consider the intricacies of reincarnation in greater detail. It is a collection of ideas, theories, and thoughts that I have come to believe about the mechanics of reincarnation—how it works, what it's trying to do, and what it all means.

Additionally, while much of this material is largely a rework of my first book, I've since come to some fresh insights and understandings of the process that were absent from my earlier work. The reader will also notice the different tenor of this work compared to my earlier

---

1. My first book about reincarnation is *Mystery of Reincarnation: The Evidence & Analysis of Rebirth* (St. Paul, MN: Llewellyn, 2005).

effort. In my previous work I attempted to present reincarnation in a balanced, objective manner. In this one, I make no such attempt at objectivity but am instead intent on demonstrating the superb rationalism that drives the entire process—a process that is quite logical once one can get past the notion of postmortem survival and acquire the ability to view the universe from a fresh perspective. That's not to say I may not play devil's advocate from time to time or present multiple hypotheses that need to be carefully weighed against each other, but let's just say that I am no longer looking to persuade my readers that reincarnation is true as much as I am interested in getting them to understand how I understand it to operate. I am content to leave it to my readers to judge whether I have been successful in this effort.

Finally, my original title for this work was *Soulquest*, for in many ways that's exactly what reincarnation is to me: the journey, or "quest," our soul takes on its path toward spiritual maturity or, as some would call it, enlightenment. It is the culmination of my own journey from cynical skeptic to believer, all designed to demonstrate how anyone—even a former hard-core Christian fundamentalist like myself—who opens themselves to spiritual truth can find that truth if they pursue it with integrity and persistence.

J. Allan Danelek
June 2009

Introduction

If anyone had told me ten years ago I would one day write a book about reincarnation, I would have laughed. Reincarnation was a foreign concept to me, one held by people who still lived in darkness. It was, from my perspective, nothing more than a pathetic effort to deny the reality and permanence of death. I was a child of the Resurrection, with Heaven as my ultimate abode. Mine was a superior faith that set me free of any notion of working out one's salvation through endless cycles of rebirth. I didn't need reincarnation. I had Jesus. That was enough.

Sometimes, however, God has a strange way of throwing you a curve. In fact, I long ago discovered it often seems to be the way He works best.

My introduction to the subject came to me quite unexpectedly, the way all intriguing ideas do. Working from the premise that a faith that refuses to ask the hard questions is a faith that is either dead or dying, one day I was scanning the library shelves in search of my next epiphany when I happened upon a simple, innocuous-looking little book by Lynn Elwell Sparrow entitled *Edgar Cayce and the Born Again Christian*.

I had heard of Cayce before. He was a psychic who had supposedly predicted the discovery of Atlantis and a modern-day Nostradamus who had managed to accumulate a small but ardent following over the years. I had assumed he was a New Ager (which I considered then to be tantamount to being a Pagan), so I was surprised to see his name next to the term *born-again Christian*. Intrigued, I took the book off the shelf and began reading the jacket copy.

The thing that caught my attention was that, at least according to Ms. Sparrow, Cayce had been a devout Christian all his life, and had often filled his readings with Christian terminology and Bible quotations. Clearly, this fact was inconsistent with what I believed a "true" Christian should be. How could a man who claimed to know Christ as his personal savior be a psychic? I wondered. It was akin to learning that the Pope was Jewish. However, I was even more surprised to find that Cayce's teachings included far more than Atlantis. While in a trance state, he also discussed at some length a subject far from my Bible-thumping heart: reincarnation.

Now, reincarnation was about as far from being a Christian concept as was sacrificing goats, and it had always been—to my understanding—relegated to the realm of the "cults." As such, it was something to be disdained and rebutted, so I was curious as to what a supposed Christian could possibly have to say about the concept. I checked out the book and took it home, confident of my ability to see through the author's thin arguments and challenge Cayce's so-called Christian beliefs.

But something else happened instead. I was impressed.

Not persuaded, exactly. Just . . . impressed. I had never seen reincarnation so thoughtfully presented from the perspective of Christianity before. While I couldn't say I bought all of Cayce's ideas, I had to admit they at least seemed well thought out. Even more surprising, I managed to learn a few things about reincarnation I had not known before. For example, I learned that the great Christian leader Origen

(c. 185–254) taught the preexistence of souls and implied a form of Christian-based reincarnation, and that reincarnation was believed in by one group of early Christians called the Gnostics. But what surprised me most was that a good percentage of professing Christians—somewhere in the neighborhood of 25 percent, according to some polls—were open to the idea of multiple rebirths as a potential postmortem possibility. Now, to a hard-core fundamentalist, such facts were more than a little disconcerting. They did, however, at least manage to get me thinking.

Intrigued, I did something dangerous for a Christian: I investigated further—not in an attempt to either prove or disprove reincarnation, but in an effort to understand why it seemed to appeal to so many people. To that end, over the next year or so I read numerous books on the subject from many different perspectives (including those of reincarnation's critics—both Christian and secular). I checked out the writings of competent psychologists and therapists who dealt with past-life regression, and I read the works of Dr. Ian Stevenson, one of the foremost experts on reincarnation, who, over the course of almost fifty years, had compiled a staggering body of work dealing with conscious past-life memories in children. I even e-mailed ministers of those faiths that taught the idea, and I was surprised to find many of my queries answered with often lengthy and thoughtful responses.

What happened next was even more catastrophic—at least from the perspective of evangelical Christianity: I came to believe it. Reincarnation provided answers for many of the tough questions I'd asked over the years and gave me a newfound perspective on eternity that has stayed with me ever since. Further, it was through understanding the process of rebirth that I came to understand much about myself, God, and my purpose here on Earth. In effect, I learned to accept reincarnation as the magnificent machine that drives the soul, and it soon became my mentor.

This discovery had a profound and far-reaching effect on me. First, it got me to reconsider my spiritual beliefs entirely, and in doing so forced me to recognize that I was playing on far too small a stage. It also got me to realize just how big God really was and that He/She/It could never be contained within the words and traditions of any holy book. But most of all what it got me to realize is that immortality really is an inherent element of our very nature that is intricately woven into the tapestry of our soul. In effect, we may incarnate into many different cultures over the eons and be a part of numerous different religious traditions, but in the end we all end up back where we started: as a divine seed experiencing itself in a hundred different guises on a very large stage that plays itself out over eternity. Quite a revelation, that.

As one who enjoys writing on paranormal themes, I naturally had to put what I'd discovered on paper. But I wanted to do more than just write another book about reincarnation. After all, there are already a number of excellent books on the subject written by men and women of exceptional credentials, but most are either case studies of past-life memories or books that tell you how to rediscover your past-life personas. There were few books, I noticed in my travels, that dealt specifically with the process of reincarnation on a theoretical level. In other words, I wanted to put together a body of work that fellow seekers like myself could go to for possible answers to the many questions we all have as to how—if this thing called reincarnation is true—it might work.

Of course, in dealing with a subject of such an esoteric nature, there are naturally many ways of looking at how the process may work, not all of which I may either be familiar with or understand sufficiently to discuss intelligently. Of those I think I do understand, however, I will endeavor to cover each of them to the best of my ability—both the rationale behind them and the inherent strengths and weaknesses of each position. We will also deal with questions concerning the nature of God, the definition of the soul, thoughts about time and space as they relate to the spiritual realm, and a number of other issues that frequently arise when any discussion of postmortem survival is undertaken. In these pages I hope that the reader will come to appreciate how reincarnation possesses an intellectual and rational consistency, one that I personally find both comforting and admirable. Of course, it's likely—in fact, it's a near certainty—that there are other hypotheses I have overlooked or dealt with in a far too superficial manner for some people's tastes, and for that I apologize. I only hope that this shortcoming will not prove detrimental in presenting a good, comprehensive foundation from which to explore the question of reincarnation further.

Finally, while I can't empirically prove that anything in this book is true, that is as it should be. Many of our beliefs must continue to rest, as always, on faith, for that is the fuel that drives us to search for ever-deeper meaning in our lives, and in so doing moves us further down the road along our own spiritual path. It is about possibilities—not only of the human spirit, but of the human heart and the hope of eternity that comprises all human philosophies and religions in their efforts to explain the inexplicable and touch upon the face of the Divine. That is our true soulquest, and the adventure we are embarked upon each day whether we realize it or not. In some small way I hope that this work will help some of you find answers, which is all that any book that attempts to speak to the question of immortality can hope to do.

chapter one

The Quest for Immortality

What happens to us when we die?

It's a question all human beings eventually ask themselves. Transcending racial, social, political, economic, and gender lines, it is the one question common to all human beings, whether we like it or not.

Yet ever since the first men and women began pondering their mortality a hundred thousand years ago, the answer has eluded us. What *does* happen when we die? What becomes of our soul, our mind, our personality—our very essence? For that matter, do we even have such a thing as a soul, or is it all an illusion we have created to give ourselves a sense of permanence and the hope of immortality? Humanity has come up with three possible scenarios to try and answer this question.

The rationalist answers this query by proclaiming that since we are nothing more than a collection of cells and our brains simply tissue encased within a mantle of bone, nothing *can* happen to us when we die. The essence, personality, mind, soul—or whatever we wish to call our consciousness—ceases to exist, endowing our time on this planet with no more meaning than that which we choose to give it during our brief sojourn here. This is, of course, also the position of the atheist, which is what makes atheism, in my opinion, so easy. It requires nothing because it offers nothing, which strikes me as a fair trade.

To most people, however, this answer is unsatisfactory. It suggests that we are little more than some great cosmic accident and that, consequently, our life has no ultimate purpose. No matter how powerful or famous or wealthy we become, for most of us, after a few generations, our name will be at best but a footnote in history, forcing us to contemplate an existence without meaning in a universe that, despite all its beauty and splendor, has no more significance—or ultimate permanence—than a flower that briefly blooms in the spring only to wither and die after a few short days of vibrant life.

I suppose there are people for whom such a prospect is acceptable. It does, after all, tidy things up and make life simply a little game we sentient beings like to play for no particularly good reason other than because we have no choice. Yet something deep within the human heart knows better. We instinctively understand that we are more than the sum of our parts, which is why most people believe their personality will survive their physical demise in some form and will continue on long after their bones have turned to dust.

This, of course, brings us to our second option, which is that the personality/ego/true self/whatever-you-want-to-call-it does survive the demise of the body to exist—at least for a time—as a separate consciousness. If this is the case, however, the next question that logically follows is what exactly happens next. Some believe, for example, that we become ghosts—little more than disembodied spirits aimlessly wandering the earth, capable of perceiving the physical realm but unable to interact with it in any meaningful way. Such people can even point to various pieces of evidence to support this contention, from reported hauntings and EVPs (electronic voice phenomena, which are otherwise inaudible voices or sounds on tape thought to be made by the dead) to automatic writing, séances, and apparent spirits caught on film.

While I have no problem with the idea of ghosts, I don't think that is truly a viable long-term option for what exactly happens to us. Ghosts have always struck me as being transitory—beings trapped on the earth plane for a time, perhaps a few months or years (with a few tarrying for decades or even centuries, according to some reports), but ultimately moving on and so essentially vanishing from our physical realm. As such, even if we are to become ghosts, it will be, at least for the vast majority of us, a brief experience and not our eternity. I suspect we all eventually move on to greener pastures, so to speak.

Now, however, is where it starts to get interesting. Most people, regardless of whether they believe in ghosts or not, believe that the essence of who we are—our soul, if you will—goes *some* place. Heaven is the favored destination for most: a place where our conscious personality, no longer shackled to the limitations and burdens of physical existence, survives within a perpetual state of bliss and joy throughout eternity. Some add to this by also embracing a belief in Hell: a perpetual state of torment for those who turn to evil and thus are doomed to exist forever within a conscious state of agony, regret, and fear.

Both positions, however, suffer from the same problem in my view, which is that they see our time here on this planet as but a blink of the eye of eternity, with the decisions we make—or fail to make—while in the body having profound and eternal ramifications. Unfortunately, this reduces the physical world to little more than a cosmic hatchery that exists only to birth new souls, each of which will spend a short amount of time in it before winging—or, potentially, plunging—to their ultimate estate. While admittedly this idea does manage to make this single life of paramount importance, it also forces one to wonder why a physical realm is necessary at all. If the physical universe exists merely as a vehicle for our creation, why couldn't the process be circumvented entirely and we be created directly into the spiritual realm, as was supposedly the case with God's angels? Why all the unnecessary pain and hardship of a physical existence—especially one in which there exists the very real danger that we might earn Hell through our misdeeds—if the spirit realm is the only destination that awaits us? In such a context, physical existence seems not only pointless, but in many ways even hazardous.

There is, however, a third position to consider. It is one that until recently has been largely ignored in the West but has been embraced by billions of people around the world for thousands of years, and that is the belief that this physical existence is neither insignificant nor transient, but instead is perpetually ongoing. It is the concept that our soul lives on not in some ethereal Eden—or Hades—somewhere, but rather that it realizes perpetual existence through a process of continual rebirths into the physical realm, making our time on this planet not one single, brief experience, but a repetitive process realized through literally hundreds of lifetimes. It is a timeless belief—one that predates both Christianity and Islam by many centuries—and one that is known by many names in many cultures. It's been called *rebirth, regeneration, transmigration of the soul,* even *metempsychosis,* but is perhaps best known to us today as *reincarnation.*

Upon first consideration, especially to those who haven't given the idea that much thought, reincarnation may be an idea that seems foreign, exotic, or even a little nonsensical—especially to the Western mind steeped in the scientific method and drenched in two thousand years of monotheistic religion. It may seem to be something for Hindu holy men to ponder, or New Agers to embrace, but nothing that seems particularly relevant to most Westerners today.

I can easily understand this perspective, for it is one I myself held for the first forty years of my life. And truth be told, it *is* an Eastern concept—one in vogue more than four millennia before Christ was born—and a belief held today by nearly two billion of the world's population, mostly in the form of Hinduism and Buddhism, making it one of the oldest and most enduring belief systems known to humanity. In fact, it may be the original postmortem belief among early humans, who probably considered the idea when they began noticing strong similarities between recently born offspring and their deceased ancestors. Perhaps the mannerisms or interests a child displayed reminded one of a deceased loved one, or a birthmark mimicked another birthmark found on a long-dead grandparent, leading village elders to imagine that the dead ancestor had returned a second time—a not unreasonable assumption in cultures that assumed the soul to be naturally immortal.

Unfortunately, Westerners have traditionally had a tendency to dismiss foreign or primordial religious concepts as "primitive" and thus reject them out of hand. However, this is slowly changing as reincarnationist beliefs make headway in the West, especially in the last fifty years, and as such beliefs become increasingly popular to ever-growing numbers of Westerners.

Actually, although relatively few people realize it, reincarnationist beliefs have always been a part of Western thought. For example, reincarnationist ideas flourished in ancient Greece almost three thousand years ago and may have played a far more extensive role in our development as a civilization than traditional histories have led us to believe. Aristotle, Socrates, Plato, and Pythagoras all taught and believed in some form of rebirth, the foundations of which were later adopted by the great Roman philosophers Ovid, Virgil, and Cicero, along with a host of other great thinkers of antiquity. In fact, some of these ideas were so prevalent in the centuries immediately preceding the birth of Christ that reincarnationist concepts played a major role in many of the "mystery" religions of the Mediterranean—religions that were themselves to become the template for other, later mystical faith systems of the region. Reincarnation, then, far from being an uncommon idea, was in fact widespread and may have strongly influenced the shape and thrust of Greek and Roman philosophy.

Even more of a surprise to many people, however, is the fact that reincarnationist concepts were also part of some of the more mystical branches of Western religion, from the Sufis of Islam to the Gnostics of the early centuries of Christianity, and even within the Hasidic and Kabbalist traditions in Judaism. In fact, at times it virtually flourished, and especially in the case of Christianity, almost became the predominant belief system, at least through the first few centuries of the church's existence—until it was forced underground by the more traditional, non-reincarnationist branches of Christianity. Few Christians today realize that it was ever a part of their own faith.

Why were reincarnationist beliefs suppressed? The obvious answer is because such beliefs threatened authority. In promising multiple rebirths, reincarnation rendered the proclamations of the Pope or the Grand Mufti or whoever was the ruling head at the time transitory and, truth be told, irrelevant. Clearly, the religious authorities were dependent upon the single-life scenario for their very livelihood, making the belief in multiple lives far too dangerous to allow to stand. As a result, reincarnation remained largely unknown outside of Asia for the better part of fifteen of the last twenty-one centuries.

Its revival in the West was imminent, however, along with the Age of Enlightenment in the eighteenth century, when the long-forgotten writings of the ancient Greeks once again became popular, and Europeans could hold to previously forbidden ideas without forfeiting their lives. Still, reincarnationist beliefs weren't widely disseminated, usually remaining in the realm of the intellectual elite and thus remaining a belief held to by only a tiny percentage of the population (although that list includes such notable figures as Dickens, Emerson, Thoreau, Shaw, Dostoyevsky, Tolstoy, Melville, Benjamin Franklin, Shakespeare, da Vinci, Kant, Dante, and Voltaire, among others).

Reincarnation finally found its way to America in a major way in the nineteenth century, but even then it did not get off to an auspicious start. First, the most vocal of its adherents was an eccentric and, some maintained, unstable woman by the name of Helena Blavatsky, who emigrated from Russia to establish the Theosophical Society in 1875. Though a woman of considerable intellect and energy, her volatility, when combined with a highly esoteric and mystical teaching style largely beyond the grasp of the average person on the street, ensured that her teachings did not find a particularly extensive audience. As such, even though she and her organization were successful in reintroducing many traditional reincarnationist beliefs to the

Western consciousness, they never managed to attract more than a tiny following, resulting in reincarnation remaining a largely foreign concept to most Americans well into the twentieth century.

That all changed in the mid-twentieth century, however, as a result of two people. The first was a simple Kentucky psychic by the name of Edgar Cayce, and the second was an unassuming Colorado house-wife named Virginia Tighe, who was to be better known to history as "Bridey Murphy." First, Cayce.

Born into poverty on a small farm near Hopkinsville, Kentucky, in 1877, Edgar Cayce did not appear destined to be a man who would in-fluence countless lives through his simple writings, but influence them he did. As a young man, Cayce accidentally discovered that he was able to put himself into self-induced trances and successfully diagnose the various ailments of the people who came to him with a variety of mala-dies, along with recommended treatments that, in many cases, proved to be remarkably effective. While that alone is curious enough, it turned out that while in these trances, he also spoke about some illnesses or dis-eases being "karmic" in nature and a byproduct of an experience from a previous lifetime. In essence, Cayce revealed nothing less than that his patients had lived previous lives on Earth, where they underwent some sort of trauma that had impacted their health in their current lifetime.

Now, the revelation that we reincarnate as a matter of course came as quite a shock to Cayce himself, who felt that as an orthodox Chris-tian such ideas were unscriptural. However, as he was intent on help-ing others, he put his doubts aside and continued to diagnose maladies in his subjects—including those resulting from traumas in their past lives—right up to the time of his death in 1945. While alive, he also was responsible for penning several books (taken from transcripts from his readings and pulled into book form by his descendents) that went into some detail as to how reincarnation worked and what it all meant. He even talked at length about the "in-between" state and how each of our various lives are recorded in a type of celestial "central library" known as the Hall of Akashic Records.[1]

Cayce's writings on reincarnation were not widely read until many years after his death, leaving the concept still little known to more than a tiny percentage of Americans. This would change a decade after the man's death, however, due to the efforts of a businessman and self-taught hypnotist named Morey Bernstein and a Pueblo, Colorado, housewife by the name of Virginia Tighe—a woman who would eventually come to be known to the world as Bridey Murphy.

It all started in November of 1952, when Mr. Bernstein, curious about the subject of reincarnation and wondering if the twenty-nine-year-old Mrs. Tighe would be able to recount a past life while under hypnosis, put the woman into a deep trance and asked her to go back in her mind, until she found herself in "some other scene, some other place, or some other time," and describe what she saw. What happened next came as quite a surprise to everyone involved: speaking in a mild brogue, Tighe identified herself as an Irish woman named Bridey Murphy and claimed to have been born in the town of Cork, Ireland, in the year 1798. Supposedly recounting a life lived in nineteenth-century Ireland, "Bridey" went on to describe in considerable detail a number of facts about her previous existence, all of it told in a lilting and progressively growing Irish accent that proved at times difficult to understand.

Intrigued by the unexpected results, Bernstein conducted five more sessions with Tighe over the next year, each of them tape recorded and witnessed by both Bernstein's wife and Tighe's husband, as well as several others. While much of what Virginia Tighe recounted was little more than anecdotal and disjointed stories from her alleged past life, some of it was detailed enough to be historically verifiable. Uncertain what to do with this information, after a few months Morey Bernstein and some journalist acquaintances hired investigators to check out "Bridey's" story. While some of the people and places the

---

1. A term or concept, however, that Cayce did not invent but that goes back to antiquity.

woman named turned out to be undocumented—record-keeping in nineteenth-century Ireland being almost nonexistent—other information was verified, and the results were published in a little book entitled *The Search for Bridey Murphy*.

Released in January of 1956, the book became an unexpected bestseller—much to both Bernstein's and Tighe's surprise—with over 170,000 copies being sold within just the first two months of its release. Bernstein's riveting account of past-life recall was even serialized in thirty-nine newspapers; an abridged version appeared in *True* magazine; 30,000 LPs of his recorded sessions were sold; and a Hollywood movie dramatizing the story was made. There was even a popular song inspired by the event, and very quickly the concept of reincarnation entered the public's consciousness in a major way.

While Tighe's story was later attacked by the scientific and religious communities and is considered by many skeptics today to have been successfully debunked,[2] there was no denying that *The Search for Bridey Murphy* was instrumental in bringing reincarnation into the mainstream of Western consciousness. Until then the concept had been held to by only a tiny fragment of the population, but after Tighe's story hit the bookstores—and despite its later debunking—interest in the subject grew dramatically. By the late 1960s, belief in reincarnation was becoming increasingly popular among the young, who, turned off by traditional Western religion and enticed by the Eastern concepts of gurus and New Age masters, had become much more open to foreign concepts and as such willing to challenge and, when necessary, abandon long-held religious dogmas when they failed to answer their questions. Moreover, the 1970s and 1980s saw a burgeoning crop of books on paranormal and occult subjects, while books by channelers—people who supposedly

---

2. The general consensus is that Virginia Tighe's memories were an example of *cryptomnesia*—a common phenomenon in which memories from the past are suppressed or forgotten only to emerge in a regression session as events from a past life. There is some debate today as to whether this was a correct appraisal of what happened, however.

act as conduits for disembodied personalities—and works by such well-known celebrities as Shirley MacLaine began to make reincarnation an increasingly acceptable belief system for many.

Reincarnationist beliefs made inroads into the scientific community as well, mostly through the work of University of Virginia psychiatrist Dr. Ian Stevenson (1918–2007), whose landmark work with children who could spontaneously recall past lives was documented in his 1966 book *Twenty Cases Suggestive of Reincarnation*. Due largely to Stevenson's work (and as a result of the nine books he was later to pen on the subject), people in the West were much more willing to look at the evidence for past lives than at any other time in history. As a result, today the subject is relatively well known to most Westerners and has been steadily gaining adherents ever since. By way of example, a 2003 Harris poll[3] found that a quarter of all Americans believe in some form of reincarnation (fully a third of non-Christians), and even many scientifically literate people, intrigued by a multitude of increasingly well-documented past-life memory cases, are willing to consider the idea. Clearly, the reincarnation genie has been let out and there seems to be no way of getting it back into its bottle.

Before we can undertake any serious investigation of how reincarnation works, however, we need to examine some of the more basic pieces of evidence frequently pointed to in support of the concept, if only to lay an important foundation from which to examine in greater detail the mechanisms that may drive it.

---

3. *The Harris Poll®* #11, February 26, 2003.

chapter two

The Evidence for Reincarnation

It's been my experience that most people who believe in reincarnation do so because it "makes sense" to them or because it answers a number of personal questions—both of which are legitimate reasons for believing in something. However, belief alone is not always enough, and understanding how reincarnation works without also understanding what makes one believe it to be true in the first place is a waste of time. Belief systems that lack solid evidence to support them are usually not worth exploring, which is why it is important to know not only *what* one believes, but also *why* one believes it. This is where solid and compelling objective evidence comes into the picture, if only so one may be able to defend one's belief system to others. To that extent, this chapter will cover—in greatly condensed form—some of the better evidence used to support reincarnation by researchers in the field today.

I recognize that many of my readers already either believe in reincarnation or are very favorably disposed to the idea, thereby potentially making this chapter unnecessary. However, I think it is always a good idea when considering any new idea that one has hard evidence from which to support one's beliefs. Those who are only interested in the mechanics of how reincarnation works and are tempted to skip this chapter and move on do so at their own risk, for it is my contention that unless one can defend one's belief in a logical and empirical way, how it might work becomes a moot point.

So, what is the evidence for reincarnation and, in the same vein, how trustworthy is that evidence, considering the intricacies of the human mind and our ability as a species to delude ourselves into believing all sorts of nonsense? Is reincarnation, as the skeptics maintain, nothing more than a collection of anecdotal stories told by highly suggestible people and, in some cases, clearly unstable personalities, or is there something more to it?

Conscious Past-Life Memories in Children

Perhaps the strongest and best-documented evidence in support of reincarnation is conscious past-life memory recall in children. More specifically, this is the phenomenon by which children as young as two years old are able to recall having lived past lives and are able to recall those lives complete with names, dates, and often the names of the villages in which they believe they previously lived. In some of the better cases, children have even visited their former homes only to be able to instantly identify members of their "former" family and provide personal details of their previous lives with uncanny accuracy. Many even recounted how they had died in that previous lifetime with a degree of certainty and knowledge inexplicable for a child.

Most of what we know of this phenomenon comes from the work of Dr. Ian Stevenson, the Virginia psychiatrist of impeccable credentials mentioned in the last chapter, who began studying cases of conscious past-life memories in children in the late 1950s. Stevenson eventually collected almost three thousand reports of such cases and personally investigated hundreds of them over the course of his life—a number of which served as sources for his exhaustive studies and appeared in his numerous articles and books.

What's most impressive about these memories is that these children had not been hypnotized or otherwise coerced into remembering previous lives, but had spontaneously exhibited conscious memories of past lives from a very early age. In fact, Stevenson specifically made it a point to ignore past-life memories acquired through hypnosis precisely because he considered such memories unreliable and fantasy prone. While children are, of course, capable of fantasizing as well, what impressed Stevenson was the wealth of personal and often intimate details the children were able to recount—details he thought unlikely a child would either imagine or learn from an adult. He believed—and many child psychiatrists concur—that children are simply not capable of retaining anything like the vast amount of information his subjects frequently provided (even after lengthy coaching), nor were their stories consistent with the type of imaginary stories children are famous for.

Even more impressive than the sheer quantity of detail the children could provide was the fact that much of it proved to be verifiable. Names often (though not always) proved to be accurate and, in most cases, turned out to be those of complete strangers to the child's current family. The children recalled former spouses, siblings, parents, and even children they had parented in their previous incarnation, and were able to describe the home they had lived in with remarkable accuracy, though they had never visited the spot during their present life. In a few cases, the children identified so strongly with their past life that they insisted on being called by their former name and even felt alienated from their present family, preferring (and, in some instances, becoming clearly upset when not permitted) to spend more time with their "previous" family—all of which makes Stevenson's work with children among the strongest evidence for reincarnation to date.

Although Stevenson was occasionally attacked for his methodology and for the fact that most of his subjects came from Asia (where reincarnationist beliefs are widespread), for the most part those who have bothered to study Stevenson's data objectively are usually impressed with his thoroughness and rigid adherence to scientific methodology.

Corresponding Birthmarks

One of the more interesting and potentially empirical pieces of evidence suggestive of reincarnation also comes from Stevenson's research. During the course of his travels he noticed that the children who claimed a violent death in a past life frequently exhibited birthmarks on their body that precisely corresponded with the fatal wounds they claimed to have suffered at the time of death. For instance, one of Stevenson's subjects, an eleven-year-old Turkish boy, recounted that in a previous incarnation he had been accidentally shot in the head with a shotgun by a neighbor. Remarkably, the boy was born with a badly deformed right ear that closely mimicked the wounds the deceased man had received, a fact later confirmed by medical records and photographs Stevenson was able to obtain from local authorities during his investigation.

And this was by no means unusual; Stevenson recounted scores of similar cases, some in which toes and fingers—and in a few cases, even entire limbs—that had been lost in a previous incarnation were missing in the current incarnation, as well as even more startling cases in which multiple birthmarks closely mimicked the precise wounds received by the past-life subject. In one case he found matching entrance and exit wounds in a subject that closely corresponded to those of the previous personality, who had died from a gunshot wound to the head, the chances of which occurring naturally would be astronomical. While not conclusive in their own right, that they defy easy natural explanation makes it more difficult for skeptics to write off such anomalies as mere coincidences, and further strengthens the case for past-life existence.

Demographic Studies

In the late 1960s another psychologist, Dr. Helen Wambach (1925–85), began a series of experiments dealing with the demographic consistency of past-life memories that produced some impressive and startling results. Intrigued by several personal experiences she had encountered when dealing with patients who had described previous lives while under hypnosis, and curious to know if there was more to it than simple imagination, Wambach decided to compare such information with anthropological, sociological, and archeological studies made of the cultures her patients had mentioned, in order to determine if there was any demographic consistency in their recounted memories.

For instance, if gender and social-class ratios proved to be inconsistent with what anthropologists and sociologists had already estimated[4] them to have been, that would demonstrate her subjects were either making up stories or inadvertently fantasizing. If, on the other hand, there proved to be a correlation with the known demographic data, that would bring significant weight to the idea that human beings continue to live on through the mechanism of multiple rebirths, for the only other possibility—that literally thousands of subjects had innocently and spontaneously manufactured demographically accurate past-life memories from their imagination—was statistically and logically untenable.

Convinced that such a study was both feasible and potentially valuable, Wambach began regressing volunteers into remembering past lives and then had them record details about their gender, race, economic status, and other often mundane specifics of their past lives. Regressing just over one thousand subjects over a ten-year period, Wambach, much to her own surprise, found that the information she obtained proved to be remarkably consistent with what demographers know of the ancient past. For instance, as the majority of Wambach's subjects were women (by about a three-to-one ratio)

---

4. Obviously, since record-keeping is a fairly modern phenomenon, demographers can only make educated guesses as to population sizes, economic status, and so on, of any particular ancient culture. However, while not precise, the numbers they produce are generally accepted as reasonable by the scientific community.

and working from the premise that most people would be unlikely to imagine themselves to have been a member of the opposite sex, there should have been a disproportionately higher number of individuals remembering themselves to have been female rather than male in a past life. Instead, Wambach discovered a biologically accurate 50/50 ratio of men to women throughout every time period. If these "memories" were based upon pure imagination, such a consistent male/female ratio should be impossible to achieve, which suggested that a high number of authentic past-life memories existed within her sample.

Other details proved to be accurate as well. Subjects frequently described architecture, clothing styles, and even coinage that was consistent with what archeologists know of the past. Even mundane details such as types of footwear, eating utensils, primary diet, and the methods used to cook food—details a would-be hoaxer would be unlikely to consider—were also consistent with the known historical record. Additionally, racial distribution and ratios proved to be correct as well, demonstrating again that either an incredibly widespread and carefully maintained hoax was afoot, or that just maybe people really do live more than one life.

Of most interest of all, the social class her subjects found themselves in proved to be remarkably consistent with most demographic studies. Wambach had her subjects recount whether they considered themselves poor, middle class, or upper class in a previous life, presuming that a disproportionate number of subjects would opt for more interesting or affluent lives, which would strongly suggest the memories were manufactured. To her surprise, however, most subjects recalled having lived rather ordinary past lives, often in desperate poverty. In fact, fewer than 10 percent of her subjects recalled living an upper-class lifestyle, and about a quarter to a third recalled being artisans or merchants (middle class) in a previous incarnation, which corresponded very closely to sociological studies from the various periods in history she covered. Her data, then, on top of demonstrating an inexplicable consistency when compared to accepted scientific expectations, also destroyed the commonly held notion that most people who recall living past lives imagine themselves to have been famous or wealthy people.

Dr. Wambach was as surprised by the results as her skeptical colleagues later proved to be, but her data seemed airtight. Though skeptics questioned her methodology (hypnotism), no one could deny that she had produced some remarkable results with her study—results that could be one of the best and most objective pieces of evidence in existence for the validity of reincarnation.

Verifiable Past-Life Memories

A fourth type of evidence for reincarnation is also the best known and most controversial—namely, those memories of a past life acquired through hypnotism that produce verifiable details (of which the Bridey Murphy case was typical). These are cases in which the subject can recall specific details of a past life while under hypnosis, especially their name or place of residence, occupations, names of spouses and family members, and other pertinent details of an alleged past life. Such verifiable memories can even be spread out over several previous incarnations, providing a treasure chest of details that can be checked against the historical record or—as in the case of Wambach's subjects—demographic studies.

Those who reject reincarnation *in toto* frequently explain away this phenomenon as being either an example of hoaxing (though confirmed cases are rare) or as the result of something called cryptomnesia (also known as lost or hidden memories)—the phenomenon by which a person recounts historical details under hypnosis gleaned not from a past life, but from a long-forgotten book or movie they may have read or seen. For the most part, however, most such memories have no easy explanation and remain among the most extensive evidence of the reality of past lives in existence.

Unfortunately, while most of these cases prove to be imbued with enough detail to make them plausible as past-life memories, none has proven to be irrefutable proof of reincarnation. There are always a few erroneous details thrown in among the verifiable facts to cast doubt on their authenticity, and so while they remain good evidence for reincarnation, they are likely to always remain just outside of the veil of being considered "proof" of reincarnation.

Xenoglossia

A handful of well-documented cases in which people reliving a past life suddenly begin speaking in a language they don't know (usually only while under hypnosis) constitutes one of the more interesting—and uncommon—pieces of evidence for reincarnation. Sometimes it can be as simple as a few foreign words or phrases or, in some instances, as complex as an entire, fluent conversation carried out in a language the subject is not even aware exists. In some of the most credible and compelling cases of xenoglossia (inexplicable use of a foreign language) recorded, the subject not only speaks in a foreign language but may even use an archaic form of it that has not been in regular usage for centuries, making it extremely unlikely to be a fantasy, a hoax, or a case of cryptomnesia. Although a good case of xenoglossia remains one of the more compelling pieces of evidence for reincarnation, such cases are so rare that they have not generated enough hard data to allow researchers to come to any conclusions.

A similar but more common phenomenon sometimes seen in past-life accounts occurs when the subject does not speak in a foreign language, but rather in a foreign dialect or accent. In other words, some subjects, while under hypnosis, break into a strong dialect they would not normally use—sometimes replete with foreign words, names, or phrases (although most of the account is still rendered in the subject's native language). A good example of this is the Irish brogue Virginia Tighe broke into when recounting her life as Bridey Murphy. However, since such accents can be learned and copied (actors are usually known for this ability), and since it's conceivable that one might inadvertently reproduce a dialect heard as a child and since forgotten, speaking in a foreign dialect will always remain problematic as evidence for a past life.

Prodigies

Another phenomenon that might be pointed to as possible evidence of reincarnation is that of children born with a natural talent or ability far beyond their years. Good examples of prodigies include Wolfgang Amadeus Mozart, who was able to compose simple arrangements of music at the age of four and compose entire symphonies by adolescence, and the seventeenth-century mathematician Blaise Pascal, who managed to outline a new geometric system by the age of eleven. That these prodigies accomplished such extraordinary achievements at such a remarkably young age could suggest their talents may have been acquired as a result of prior knowledge, presumably during a past life (a prospect that even Mozart himself claimed was the reason behind his remarkable abilities).

This does seem to suggest that a lifetime of learning can somehow survive death and manifest itself in the next incarnation. The problem, however, is that if previous knowledge can be brought into a fresh incarnation, why doesn't it happen more often? As there are many people who possessed great knowledge and skills in the past, child prodigies should be reasonably common, yet in reality such gifted children are rare, which seems to suggest other, more prosaic reasons for such early ability.

However, one possibility does present itself, at least from a reincarnationist perspective. It should be recognized that only recently have there been such large numbers of scientists, musicians, artists, and academicians on the planet; in past centuries such people were comparatively rare. As such, there would have been a very small "pool" of highly knowledgeable (or academic) souls out there looking to reincarnate, making prodigies uncommon. Additionally, some prodigies may be born into a third-world culture in which such innate skills lie dormant and undiscovered, and it is even possible that only some souls are capable of transferring knowledge gained in one lifetime into the next or that it may be done only in special cases for specific reasons.

While child prodigies are rare, however, gifted children are not. Everyone knows children who are especially quick learners and seem to operate on a higher academic level than their peers. Could it be that those children we consider gifted or especially bright were actually educated individuals in a past life who, while no longer retaining the specific knowledge they held in that earlier incarnation, still retain the habit of learning they acquired then? The knowledge itself may not survive, but perhaps simply the *desire* to learn is the residual echo of an educated past life. Could that explain the apparent disparity we see in our educational system, where some students seem to excel while others struggle or drop out entirely?[5]

Déjà Vu

Have you ever had the strange feeling that you're repeating an experience you're certain you've never had before or entering a building that seems strangely familiar to you, though you know for a fact you've never been there? If so, you have experienced what is referred to as déjà vu—the phenomenon of repeating an event or having inexplicable knowledge of a place you've never previously visited.

To some people, such experiences are considered evidence of a past life—an "echo" or ill-defined memory that has somehow survived the rebirthing process, only to be inadvertently "triggered" by some event in the present. It can be as simple as a subtle sense that you've had a particular conversation or experience before—much

---

5. Of course, parenting and environment are also factors in determining a child's scholastic capabilities, although academically astute children sometimes hail from dysfunctional homes in which education is marginalized or ignored. Perhaps it's not so much one's intelligence that emerges from an educated past life, but rather a love of learning that marks a previous academic tradition.

like the feeling one gets when reading a book one has read before but can't recall when—or as extraordinary as knowing the precise layout of a building or even an entire town that one has never visited before.

Science insists that what we call déjà vu is simply a coincidental similarity between a present experience and a similar but forgotten past experience. For example, someone may feel a special familiarity with a house he has never before visited, not because he lived there in a previous life but because he has at one time or another visited a similar home that unconsciously reminds him of this one. And how many of us have not from time to time had a conversation that we've long since forgotten that is inadvertently repeated in the present? Memory is a tricky affair that is capable of playing all sorts of pranks on us.

However, this possible solution does little to explain the sheer amount of detail that is sometimes recalled in the best cases of déjà vu. Even a similarity of places or events cannot explain, for instance, how a man can correctly describe the maze of streets that lie just ahead in a small village he is visiting for the first time, nor does it seem to comfortably account for how a woman can recall with un-erring exactitude the precise layout of a home she had never seen before. A similarity with places or things experienced in the past can go only so far; at some point, the odds against correctly guessing the street layout of a city or the location of various rooms within a sprawling mansion become astronomical.

Socio-Psychological Evidence for Reincarnation

While they lack the sort of empirical—that is, testable—characteristics of xenoglossia, a past-life memory, and other such evidence for reincarnation, there are other types of evidence that might also suggest past lives. Additionally, this evidence is more evident in our day-to-day world and is of a type we are more likely to encounter than déjà vu or spontaneously recalled past lives.

If we work from the premise that reincarnation is true, it should affect us in ways both obvious and subtle in many areas of our life, such as through the outward nature of our personality and personal perceptions. In other words, if we retain anything at all from a past life, those experiences should shape our current understanding, beliefs, tastes, and tendencies to some degree—in much the same way that the experiences from our childhood shape those things in our adult life.

Of course, some—if not most—of our personal characteristics can be explained by our environment and upbringing, but too often we find ourselves sharing an environment with siblings or acquaintances and still emerge as very different people from them. The fact that two siblings can grow up in nearly identical circumstances within the same household only to take two very different paths upon reaching adulthood is a mystery of human behavior; that one is extroverted and has a good head for business while the other is shy and has a remarkable aptitude for music cannot be easily explained away with either genetics or upbringing—which suggests some third element is at work, forging very different personalities from what is essentially the same raw material. Obviously, this would be a far more introspective and subjective search for evidence of a past life, but, if we are open to the idea, it is the type each of us can find if we take the time to search our own life for the telltale clues that reincarnation may have left.

Personality

Most people are aware of the often vast differences in personality evident among even the closest siblings. But what is it that determines our personalities? Why are some of us naturally more patient than others, and why do some of us enjoy reading while others would never consider cracking a book? Moreover, why are some of us drawn to museums and art galleries while others are drawn with equal passion to shopping malls and sporting events? In effect, why do children often emerge from the womb with very different and distinct characteristics—characteristics that emerge long before the child is old enough to experience anything that could conceivably shape his or her personality? Do we explain it in terms of chemical reactions in the brain, environmental factors, or even genetic proclivities? Or, as some reincarnationists believe, are we simply a reflection of our soul's own basic personality, reflecting its basic attributes and characteristics through each new incarnation in the same way an actor's basic personality often manifests itself in each role he plays?

Hobbies, Interests, and Obsessions

Could our hobbies and interests also be an "echo" from a previous incarnation? For example, if someone was an artist in a past life, might that person not be drawn toward expressing himself through drawing and painting in this life as well? Is a Civil War buff simply pursuing a new interest, or is he in some ways still clinging to a past incarnation in which he was a participant in that war?

Reincarnation, while not the only possible explanation, must at least be considered, especially in those cases where one develops a hobby or interest that seems out of place (such as a boy growing up in landlocked Iowa developing a fascination for eighteenth-century schooners or an Australian housewife captivated by life in Tsarist Russia). Later in this book we will explore an authentic case in which a hobby that came to border on an obsession may have had its basis in a possible past life, but for now it is enough to be aware of how much of our past may manifest itself in our present, albeit in the most subtle and subconscious ways.

Phobias

The human tendency to develop unusual and often overwhelming fears of things that do not constitute a genuine danger is a common phenomenon almost everyone has experienced at one time or another.

How one acquires a phobia is a well-understood process; they are the result of some trauma or event from one's past that manifests itself in later life as a panic-inducing fear. For example, a boy who nearly drowns may develop an unnatural fear of water, or a girl who was thrown from a horse as a child may have an irrational fear of horses in later life. As such, phobias of one kind or another affect most people, though usually they are mild enough that they do not seriously impact a person's life.

But what of those phobias that seem to develop *without* an accompanying trauma to explain them? For example, a therapist may find that a man who suffers from an irrational fear of water has never experienced or witnessed a drowning in his life, making his phobia irrational. Does this not raise the question, then, of whether such a fear was acquired as a result of a trauma experienced in a past life?

While not proof of past lives (or past-life traumas), such incidents do force us to ask ourselves whether many of the things we fear—especially those fears and phobias that seem out of place and far more severe than might seem reasonable—are but mere echoes from a distant past.

Homosexuality and Transgenderism

Until fairly recently it was assumed that homosexual behavior was a freely chosen lifestyle choice that could be resisted with sufficient willpower, but evidence has subsequently shown that same-sex attraction may also have a genetic link. Yet what would cause such a proclivity, especially considering the negative consequences such a lifestyle "choice" has traditionally incurred in most societies? Is same-sex attraction a question of environment and upbringing, or is it entirely a matter of biology?

Or could there be another factor involved? What if the underlying cause of homosexuality is neither environmental nor genetic, but is instead the result of a previous opposite-sex incarnation? Since regression therapists frequently encounter cases of men remembering having been a woman in their immediate past life—and women of having been a man—could cross-gender reincarnation have a more profound impact than might be expected? In essence, is it possible that in identifying so closely with their previous gender that some men and women may retain many of the affinities they possessed in their last incarnation? In effect, could a man be attracted to other men because he still perceives them from the perspective of a woman, as a result of having been a woman in his last life? While far from irrefutable evidence for reincarnation, it does seem to answer a few questions rather nicely.

Of course, if true, this doesn't answer why more people don't experience an orientation for same-gender attraction, especially if crossing genders from incarnation to incarnation is not all that uncommon. Also, it doesn't deal with the issue of bisexuality, or crossdressing in heterosexuals. However, while the entire issue of human sexuality is a complex one, is it possible that some sexual tendencies are the result of a *partially* successful gender shift but not a *completely* successful one? In other words, when souls move from one gender to the other, is it possible that the new personality the soul has generated needs time to reacquaint itself to its new sexuality, resulting in a degree of gender confusion? If one had lived several incarnations as a man and was suddenly reincarnated as a woman, one might be forgiven for imagining the process to be something less than simple.

This is not to suggest that homosexuals or bisexuals are "flawed" in some way, or that experiencing life from the perspective of a gay or bisexual person doesn't have benefits in terms of spiritual growth. It is simply to suggest that reincarnating may not be an easy, effortless, or flawless process.

Along the same lines, could our past-life sexual experiences be reflected in this incarnation in other ways as well? In effect, could a person who was sexually brutalized in a past life enter this life in the form of a serial rapist, or could promiscuity in one lifetime be passed on to the next (or even result in an irrational fear of, or even disgust for, sexual activity in the present life)? For that matter, could those who choose a celibate lifestyle be doing so in an effort to counter a promiscuous past life, or could a promiscuous present be the result of a repressed sexuality in a previous incarnation? One's past-life sexual experiences—as is true of all life experiences—may have more to say about one's present practices, preferences, and attitudes than we can possibly imagine.

Conclusions

Although none of these pieces of evidence is, in and of itself, irrefutable evidence of reincarnation, when combined they do seem to indicate that this single life we are living now may be neither the first nor the last, but merely the most recent. Additionally, they even suggest that we may not be so different from our "old" selves as we imagine. We may be different manifestations of the same soul, separated only by the limitless expanses of time and space, but deep down inside we may remain essentially the same person.

But despite this impressive evidence and the general revival of interest in reincarnation evident in our world today, it has been my experience that most people still perceive reincarnation as a purely New Age belief or, worse, a "tabloid" faith with no more substance than astrology, tarot cards, and healing crystals, resulting in it generally being relegated to the back room of Western thought. I suspect, however, that the reason for this is simply because few people really understand what it is or how it really works. Unfortunately, this lack of understanding makes it almost impossible to understand how spirituality works in any practical sense, for reincarnation is the mechanism that not only drives spiritual growth but also makes it possible in the first place. As such, let's explore the mechanics of reincarnation from a Western perspective in an effort to determine not only what it is trying to do, but how it goes about accomplishing that task. In other words, how, exactly, does this thing called reincarnation work?

chapter three
The Purpose of Reincarnation

Most people understand that reincarnation is simply the process by which a person is reborn into a new body sometime after they die, in a never-ending cycle of birth-death-rebirth. What is less clear to many, however, is precisely *why* a person does this, especially considering how difficult life can sometimes prove to be.

Most people assume we do this in order to learn certain lessons (or perhaps to relearn the lessons we failed to grasp in a previous lifetime), while to others it's a means of balancing some sort of cosmic scale of justice by having us pay off some "sin debt" we've acquired through evil actions we've committed in past lifetimes. In fact, these two positions—in some form or another—are probably held by 99 percent of reincarnationists worldwide, with the former position dominating Western thought and the latter being more consistent with Eastern belief systems.

While I can appreciate how someone could come to embrace either position—or even attempt to merge them—I believe they are, if not incorrect, at least incomplete. To see why I make such a statement, let's look for a moment at each rationale and see how well they hold up in the light of reason. Since this book is written mainly with a Western audience in mind, let's start with the most commonly understood purpose behind reincarnation—namely, that the soul is here to learn.

Life as a Classroom

The idea that life is a classroom where we learn all sorts of lessons that we will then—one hopes—take into our next incarnation seems almost self-evident to most people, and therefore is usually assumed to be the primary rationale behind reincarnation. After all, life itself is a learning process, so it's easy to imagine reincarnation as being a means by which we expand our knowledge and mature spiritually as well.

But what kinds of things are we learning, and if we are supposed to bring them into future incarnations, why do we have trouble recalling them from one incarnation to the next? In other words, how can I work on some problem area in my life—racism, intolerance, anger, etc.—if I don't remember how these areas negatively impacted my last life? I have to admit that the fact we don't remember our past lives has been one of the best pieces of ammunition used by skeptics to challenge the concept, and was a big stumbling block for me in embracing reincarnation for many years. After all, it seems obvious that if reincarnation is to have any value in developing us spiritually, it would seem that recalling our past lives would be imperative, for otherwise what value is there in the hard lessons learned in a past life? For that matter, doesn't the entire process become an obscene waste of time if we end up repeating the same mistakes because we don't remember having made them before? Isn't that simply experiencing things for the sake of experiencing them, with no long-term benefits?

This is a valid point, but it fails to explain precisely what reincarnation is trying to do. The purpose of reincarnating is not simply to recall our past errors so that we might avoid making the same mistakes again, but to grow spiritually. Paradoxically, a part of that growth process may include *making the same mistakes over again*. In essence, it may actually be *necessary* we forget our past lives—along with both their mistakes and successes—if we are ever truly to learn anything from them.

However, this makes it sound as if each incarnation *is* a learning experience after all, and to some degree that is true. Yet this isn't learning in the traditional sense (by which we acquire information, retain it, and use it to make better future decisions) but more a process of spiritual maturation. While the two can be difficult to differentiate—after all, maturity often comes about as a result of numerous life experiences—they are not one in the same. In the same way that wisdom may be a natural byproduct of the experiences we've endured while on this planet without it being the reason we are here, spiritual maturation is a natural byproduct of enduring multiple incarnations without being the reason for reincarnation. In other words, while we may not retain conscious memories of a past life, we may still retain the underlying lessons those past-life experiences taught us. For instance, we may not recall the process by which we acquired patience, but we retain the benefit of that process in this lifetime regardless. Past-life experiences, then—while absent from our current consciousness—are retained on a deeper "soul level" where they can be carried over from one incarnation to another. While the specific details of each past-life lesson may be lost, it's only because they aren't important; it is the end result that reincarnation is interested in, not the process by which we get there.

This process, by the way, also explains why we don't recall precise knowledge from previous incarnations (such as knowing anatomy as a result of having been a doctor in our last life). While at first thought it would seem to be advantageous to retain the accumulated knowledge of a hundred past lives, it would be more likely that such a capacity would turn out to be a problem. For example, imagine how much more a modern doctor knows about medicine than did his nineteenth-century counterpart. As such, were his nineteenth-century counterpart to reincarnate in the twenty-first century with his medical knowledge intact, such knowledge—in being so out of date—might prove to be not only a hindrance to being a proficient, modern doctor, but it might even prove dangerous. While the earlier medical knowledge might perhaps prove to be helpful, more likely it is going to be detrimental, at least in the near term.

As such, it appears that we are far better off coming into each incarnation largely unaware of what our previous incarnation experienced or knew. In effect, we are better off coming from the womb with a clean slate—so to speak—thereby making each new lifetime a fresh opportunity to start anew. Of course, that's not to say that past-life knowledge may not influence aspects of our current incarnation, but even if it were to do so, it seldom seems to impact it in any significant way. In fact, more frequently it appears that instead of building upon past-life knowledge, we simply move on to other areas of interest and pursue careers largely unrelated to those we experienced in a past life. Which is why people who were doctors or musicians or barrelmakers in their last incarnation seldom become doctors or musicians or barrelmakers in this life. They may retain an interest in medicine or music, or even a curiosity about how barrels are made, but rarely is one lifetime a continuation of a previous one.

Most reincarnationists who hold to this "life as a classroom" concept do not maintain that reincarnation is about refining or enhancing previous knowledge, but instead they believe it is about retaining the spiritual lessons gained in a previous incarnation so that we might continue to grow spiritually in this one. In other words, we might learn a huge degree of self-control during a particular lifetime or perhaps overcome a severe gambling addiction, the lessons of which we take into our current incarnation, providing us with a degree of self-control that would be impossible to achieve without such experiences.

However, and while admittedly this idea does have merit, it suffers from many of the same problems as the "retaining knowledge" prospect, in that since we don't normally retain conscious memories from our previous incarnations, we can't retain what spiritual lessons we might have gained from whatever experiences we had in that past life. While past spiritual lessons may, to some degree, shape the direction our present experiences take, there is no solid evidence that we really ever learn from our success or our failures from one incarnation to another, largely because we don't remember having made them; and once they are forgotten, their ability to teach is lost—at least on a conscious level.

A further point to consider is that if we were able to recall our past lives in perfect clarity and knew who we had been in our last life, and could see the world through those eyes anew, we would not be experiencing a new life but merely continuing a previous incarnation in a new body. As such, it is important to the process that each time we reincarnate, our memory and, for that matter, our previous personality—with all its idiosyncrasies, quirks, mannerisms, knowledge, and perceptions, and with a lifetime of memories and experiences—disappear. Much like a chalkboard is erased at the end of each school day in order to prepare for the next day's lessons, so too our "chalkboard" must be wiped clean so we may start our lessons afresh.

Finally, consider for a moment how problematic past-life memories have proven to be to those people who claim to experience them. Often the memories are so traumatic that such people require psychiatric counseling to overcome them, and they can even prove to be an impediment in other ways to those who suffer from a type of "post-rebirth syndrome." This is why pre-incarnate or past-life memories are generally bad: they prevent one from moving toward spiritual maturity until and unless they first deal with their past-life trauma. By way of an example, imagine that a man who was brutally tortured and murdered in a previous incarnation is so traumatized by the event that he lives out his present life in a perpetual state of fear. Terrified of people and unwilling to leave the safe confines of his home or interact with others in any meaningful way, he is incapable of moving on to other lessons he needs to learn in this lifetime in order to grow spiritually. If such a person is fortunate, he may receive therapy to deal with these fears, but it may take years before progress is made. Plus, of course, there are those who never seek help for their traumas at all and so are entirely stymied in their efforts to grow beyond their fears. In such cases, then, a past-life memory has become a hindrance to the growth process and can, in fact, stop it completely if not purged from the conscious memory. The problem, then, lies not in failing to recall past-life memories, but in failing to rid our psyche of *all* of them.

Karmic Justice

As for the second rationale for reincarnation—that each life is designed to work off the sin debt acquired from an earlier one (or, as some believe, that a life of ease may be a reward for a virtuous past life)—it too fails to pass the test of logic. For people to suffer for the sins of a past incarnation—an incarnation that they have no conscious memory of—is akin to being hanged for the crimes your grandfather committed a century ago. No matter how "evil" (however one cares to define the term) you may have been in a past life, there simply is no absolution to be realized in being punished for it in this life. Such ideas are a byproduct of the human insistence that justice be served as well as the human propensity toward guilt and remorse, which is what makes this rationale so appealing to millions of people (and drives the inhumane caste system of Hinduism). But how does punishing the present personality for the crimes committed by a past personality undo those crimes, bring restitution, or otherwise change the circumstances that drove those acts? As such, to punish the current personality for the crimes of the past is futile; without some context within which to demonstrate that a punishment was truly earned, it is a pointless exercise in condemnation.

By way of example, let's say that "Cutthroat Jack"—an archetypal criminal from the Old West—was captured and lynched by a posse in 1889, only to be reincarnated in the body of a baby boy named Fred in 1913. Now, karma would have us believe that Fred, in unwittingly being the reincarnation of the hated and feared outlaw, must suffer for the crimes of Jack, resulting in a life that seems for all practical purposes "snake-bit" from the beginning. Aside from suffering from a badly deformed right leg—the same leg, incidentally, that old Jack once took a bullet in—throughout the course of his life, he also sees his parents murdered in a botched robbery and his fiancée raped and killed by a previous and spurned suitor, and finally sees his own hard-earned savings stolen by an unscrupulous business partner. Broken and destitute, Fred eventually dies from alcoholism at the age of thirty-five, in 1948, his emaciated corpse discovered in a decrepit shack many weeks after his death.

From the perspective of karmic or "punitive" reincarnation, Fred, being the reincarnation of Cutthroat Jack, got exactly what he deserved for his previous evil deeds. In fact, almost everything that happened to him perfectly corresponded to the actions Jack had been guilty of in his life—murder, rape, and theft being only the most heinous of the many crimes he had committed during his brief reign of terror. By experiencing the painful consequences of the actions carried out by his previous personality, it is assumed Cutthroat Jack—even in the guise of Fred—will better be able to understand the enormity of his crimes and give the soul that generated Jack the chance to atone for its sins.

Of course, the problem is that Fred is *not* Cutthroat Jack—at least in the practical sense—for he is a uniquely separate personality completely removed from his past-life persona. Since he has no recollection of his past incarnation and has done nothing in his present life to warrant punishment, from his limited perspective he is not experiencing the consequences of his previous crimes but is simply suffering one calamity after another until he is finally left a broken man. He can't perceive the misfortunes that come upon him as a lesson, but instead sees them purely as a series of horrible and inexplicable miscarriages of justice. There is no means by which he might understand the lessons karma is trying to teach him, nor can he appreciate the need that his past crimes be offset by his current suffering. It's akin to waking one morning in a wretched dungeon and being told you are to remain there the rest of your life for a crime you have absolutely no recollection of committing. With no memory of the crime, the punishment can never have the effect of serving justice.

Yet from the perspective of retributive reincarnation, none of that is important. It is the soul that is being punished for its crimes, not the personality it manifests. What particular incarnation it happens to find itself in at any given time is beside the point—justice will be served regardless. From this perspective, then, there is no injustice in Fred's horrific life and, in fact, it would all be seen as part of a greater, perfect plan.

Unfortunately, it is not the eyes of the soul that we see through in this life, but through the eyes of the personality through which the soul has manifested. Even if we accept that the punishment may be—at least theoretically—justified, the personality that is actually experiencing the consequences of that punishment is suffering for a crime it did not commit, but is guilty of only by association. Just as we would consider imprisoning a son for the crimes of his father to be profoundly unjust, so too should this scenario be rejected as patently unfair and, in fact, entirely in opposition to any concept of a loving God.

Finally, this logic also applies for being rewarded in this life for a good and virtuous past life: just as it makes no sense for an undeserving man to be punished for the crimes of a past life, why should the universe bestow upon anyone something that person has not truly earned? It is a bit like inheriting your father's millions though you did nothing to earn it and may be utterly undeserving of such wealth. We will examine the question of karma in some detail later in the book, but for now it is enough to see that the whole notion of a universe built upon some great scale of justice is not only impractical but probably unworkable.

An Evolving Soul?

Of course, learning lessons and paying off karmic debt are not the only two rationales provided to explain why we reincarnate. Another rationale that has been suggested is that the soul reincarnates as a means of evolving or, more accurately, maturing toward perfection, which is an idea that may have some merit. After all, reincarnationists consistently suggest that souls move in an upward direction from immaturity to ever-increasing levels of maturation, producing correspondingly more mature personalities in the process, until the soul finally achieves perfection. In fact, it is taught by some schools of thought that achieving this perfection is what finally breaks the rebirth cycle.

Basically, the idea works along the lines that while a soul may not be punished for the indiscretions of a previous incarnation, it may *choose* to experience certain circumstances through which it may learn from its previous experiences. For example, a person who was a racist in one life may choose to come back as a member of the very race she previously despised, all in an effort to understand the negative repercussions that racism possesses. While this may sound similar to karmic retribution (an evil victimizer returning as an innocent victim so as to appreciate the impact his evil had), it's not exactly the same thing. First, unlike karmic retribution, it would be voluntary rather than mandatory, and, second, it is designed to expand one's perspective rather than punish one for previous crimes.

Admittedly, this "evolving soul" scenario can look very similar, but the idea here is quite different. To return to our example of Cutthroat Jack, he would not incarnate into a man named Fred and then suffer the very same crimes others suffered at Jack's hand, but instead the soul that had generated Fred might choose to be born into a life that would be more enriching to others in an effort to offset the cruelty and brutality wrought in the previous incarnation. Perhaps Cutthroat Jack's soul would choose to incarnate into a man who chooses to become a sheriff so he might protect people from the very type of person he was in his last life, or perhaps someone who works with prisoners in rehabilitating them. In any case, nothing that the soul chooses would be designed to make up for past sins but instead would be done in an effort to turn those negatives into something positive, and therefore mature as a soul.

However, this concept suffers from many of the same problems as karmic retribution, in that even if Fred does pursue a more positive venue in his next life in an effort to offset the negative impact of having been Cutthroat Jack, in not remembering having been the outlaw, how does he learn from his new experience? The answer is that he doesn't, at least not in the way we think of learning as being a byproduct of changing direction in response to previous failures. Instead, the reincarnation as beneficent Fred is chosen by the soul, which *does* recall the previous incarnation even if the personality we call Fred does not. In other words, the incarnation as Fred is a result of the soul's ongoing maturation and not some effort to either suffer for or undo the evils of the past. It is simply the soul demonstrating it is growing up—so to speak—with each subsequent incarnation being realized through ever more enlightened personalities.

Defining Perfection

The main problem with this concept is that it implies the soul is not fully mature from the beginning and that the goal of reincarnation is to achieve spiritual perfection. However, both premises are flawed, because the soul is already inherently perfect *exactly the way it is*. In other words, we are not here to *achieve* perfection, because perfection is *what we already are* —at least on a spiritual level—as a byproduct of our inherent divine connection.

I know this sounds unlikely. We aren't used to perceiving our-selves—or anything for that matter—as "perfect" under even the most generous definition of the word. In our culture the term has come to mean the complete absence of error or mistake. In the usual use of the term, for anything to be perfect it has to be flawless, and since we don't generally consider perfection to be a realistic option in a human being, the entire statement sounds ludicrous.

However, that is a very human understanding of the term. The con-cept of inherent perfection is not really such a stretch if we genuinely consider what the term "perfect" *really* means. In actuality, *something is perfect simply by being and doing what it was designed to be and do.* In other words, everything is already perfect the way it is.

Again, a difficult concept to embrace. But consider for a moment just what it means: a fleecy white cloud floating lazily through an azure sky on a bright, sunny day is, for all intents and purposes, per-fect. It may not be the largest cloud or the most dazzling, but in terms of what it was meant to be—a simple collection of water vapor—it *is* perfect. The lion hunting for game in an African savannah, a seal sunning itself on a warm rock, a child doing his or her arithmetic, a stone, a tree, a blade of grass—each is perfect in their own way. In fact, if we really look at the world through the eyes of a child, the imperfect world we imagine to exist all around us is actually filled with perfection. Of course, the lion may fail to make a kill and the child may err while trying to find the sum of two numbers, but each is being precisely what they are supposed to be.

"Perfection," then, as a measure of flawlessness, is a purely human invention; we may rave over the "perfect" Christmas tree, but that is an arbitrary designation we assign it only because it happens to have a nice form and we find it personally pleasing to the eye. It would be equally as perfect were it misshapen and lopsided, for it is still exactly what it was intended to be—a tree. Perfection is achieved when some-thing is or does precisely what it was designed to do. A piece of music that expresses the particular mood the composer was going for or a work of art that captures the raw emotion of the artist's innermost being in precise clarity are perfect, for they have done exactly what they were designed to do. Even a carpenter's trusty hammer—dented and scratched as it may be by many years of use—is perfect for the same reason, in that it fulfills the role it was designed for.

In the same way, then, the soul is already perfect and, in a sense, each personality it creates—as far as it is a tool for growth—is also perfect regardless of whether we may consider it flawed or even evil from a human perspective. As a result, the soul cannot reach for perfection, for it already is precisely that as a result of being and doing what it was designed to be and do. In effect, there is no level of perfection to shoot for, just as the man born into great wealth has no need to aspire to be rich. The soul is perfect just the way it is.

The True Purpose of Reincarnation

So, if reincarnation is not a means to learn, to realize some sense of universal justice, or to evolve toward perfection, then what *is* its purpose?

The answer is deceptively simple and yet tremendously complex: since the soul cannot *achieve* perfection because it already *is* perfection, it can *realize* that perfection by forgetting that it is perfect and instead experiencing itself as something other than perfect.

I know that sounds contradictory. How does a soul experience its own perfection by experiencing imperfection? To answer that, ask yourself: What is the quickest way to experience good health? Simple: become sick. Only in lacking naturally good health are you able to experience what it is to be healthy. Only by living in poverty can you truly understand what wealth is. Only by living in darkness, in a world where hatred, anger, violence, and war exist in all their many manifestations, can you come to appreciate love, joy, and peace. Only by being that which you are not naturally can you come to know what you are in reality—to know yourself, so to speak. That is the purpose of reincarnation. It is the soul's attempt to *know itself*, which it does by undergoing a series of lives in human or, at the very least, sentient form on this planet or on others.

But why should the soul need or even want to undergo this often painful journey? What is the payoff, so to speak, that it hopes to realize by enduring this countless progression of lifetimes, sometimes under extreme conditions of poverty, sickness, and oppression? To answer that, it is first necessary to understand what, precisely, the soul *is*, for only in doing that may we come to understand its agenda.

chapter four
Defining the Soul

I suspect that most people believe they understand what the soul is—even if they may not personally believe they have one themselves. However, I've discovered that, like the word *God*, the word *soul* tends to be defined in many ways, making it important that we nail down a single definition so we can understand the process of rebirth in a more consistent manner.

In basic terms, the soul is the energy of our essence or, more simply, our true self. It is that part of us that exists outside of and apart from the body, and is both inherently immortal and eternal. It is the single element of ourselves that transcends our human experiences while at the same time reflecting those experiences back into each new experience we take on. It is more than mere intellect and personality but is, in effect, the very heart of who we are as a person, with all our dreams, wisdom, humor, compassion, and love intact. The soul is who we are on the inside, not what we want others to see on the outside; it is the true us, stripped of all pretense and role-playing.

The problem is that even if we can agree that the soul is the non-physical aspect of ourselves, that still doesn't tell us precisely *what* it is. Where does it come from? What is it made of? Is it a created thing, or is it a part of something much larger than itself?

To Western religion, the soul is generally considered a created "thing" that is brought into existence by God to animate His creation. As such, it is not usually considered eternal (that is, it has not always existed), and—according to some philosophies—it may not even be necessarily immortal, though this is the minority view. Normally, it is generally thought to exist in either a state of eternal bliss—Heaven— or within a world of darkness and regret—Hell—after leaving the earthly plain, though there are also those who believe the disembodied soul exists within a type of perpetual, unconscious limbo world or perhaps within some sort of dream state. Some even imagine it remains tied to the physical realm in some capacity—at least for a time—to exist as a type of ghostly entity.[6]

Within Eastern concepts, however, the soul is not simply some ball of created, conscious energy floating about in linear time and space, but an integral part of something larger and far more vast than we can begin to imagine. To the Hindu, the soul is a part of the *Brahman*, which is understood to be the principle and source of the universe—a type of divine intelligence that pervades all beings, including the individual soul (or *atman* in Eastern thought). The soul, then, could be compared to a wave on the ocean; while tiny in comparison to the vast ocean around it, it remains a separate but integral part of the much larger body of water. In effect, then, the soul is a small part of what we might call God in Western thought, making the human soul nothing less than an extension of God. In fact, it *is* God, collectively speaking, in the same way that all the water molecules in the ocean collectively make up the ocean.

---

6. Within Christianity is a belief that the soul is not inherently immortal, but must be given immortality by God, usually as a reward for proving itself worthy of such an honor. This position is known as *annihilationism,* and though not a majority view, it remains an important element of Christian teaching. However, for the most part it is safe to assume that among those who believe in a soul, not only is it generally considered an important aspect of sentient life, but there are as many opinions of what becomes of the soul after death as there are religions.

Of course, to the Western mind such a position is usually considered blasphemous or, at the very least, confusing. The soul may be similar in nature to the Creator, many will argue, but it is still considered a separate element apart from God that, while being formed "in the image" of God, would not be considered an integral part of God—much less God in both essence and nature. That would be taking the definition too far, at least to some.

However, to understand reincarnation it is necessary that the soul's relationship to the Divine be firmly established, for it is this relationship that is the rationale and, indeed, the mechanism behind rebirth. To divorce the soul from its source is to miss the entire point of the exercise. While it's entirely possible for a created, individualized soul of the Western variety to reincarnate—perhaps for the purpose of purging itself of the last vestiges of sin and thus become at last worthy of being in the Creator's presence—it is in understanding the soul from the Eastern perspective that pulls the concept together in a cohesive manner. As such, before we can go any further with our discussion, it is first necessary to rethink how we define God, for since the soul and the Divine are intricately linked, to understand the one is to understand the other.

I realize I'm treading on sacred ground here, and the concept of God I introduce in these pages may be entirely too alien for many to accept. But even those who are unwilling to accept the Eastern definition of divinity can still come away with a good working knowledge of how I believe the process is supposed to work. At a minimum, it should at least give the reader an appreciation for how varied and diverse the definition of God can be, forcing us to appreciate the rich tapestry of tradition that makes up the belief systems of the planet's seven billion residents.

God: A Study in Contrasts

Perhaps one of the most surprising aspects of reincarnation is that one doesn't need to believe in God to believe in reincarnation! The adherents of Jainism in India do not believe in God at all, but rather they imagine that souls perpetually move in and out of physicality with no particular purpose in mind. To them, the soul has always existed and always will exist, and so it requires no originating source nor a particular purpose behind reincarnation beyond it simply being the process by which we exist.

It's probably safe to say that most reincarnationists do believe in God, although, as is the case with differing definitions of the word *soul*, how various reincarnationists define the term may vary widely. At the risk of greatly oversimplifying things, there are two basic ways of perceiving God. The first—and the one most comfortable to the Western mindset—is known as the "transcendent" God. In this concept, God is perceived as a spirit or personality that exists outside of, and apart from, "His" (and God is invariably thought of in masculine terms within most Western traditions[7]) creation like some great benevolent monarch overseeing a vast kingdom. He is thought to be a conscious, moral agent of unlimited power and intellect that, though existing entirely apart from time and matter, uses both in His ongoing quest to create and, when necessary, destroy. He is "first cause" or, more precisely, that from which everything else emanates, and there is nothing that exists that He did not first conceive of and create through the sheer power of His will. To such a God, the universe was brought into existence in the distant past and will end at some future date, at which point time will come to an end and the great "experiment" will be concluded.

The second concept about God held by a substantial percentage of the world's population is what might be called the "immanent" God. From this perspective, to speak of God is to refer to all that is, all that

---

7. Westerners commonly refer to God using masculine pronouns, whereas those who follow Eastern religions would find such a gender-specific identity to be limiting. For the sake of clarity, I will generally refer to God as "He," though there may be points at which I use a gender-neutral identity when speaking of God in a non-religious context.

has ever existed, and all that ever will exist. God is not a someone or a something that creates things out of nothingness, but rather God *is* the creation itself—every molecule, every cell, and every atom in the universe are all a part of the vast and infinite "body" of God. It is eternal and immortal, has always existed and will always exist, without beginning or end. To the Eastern mind, then, God does not "bring forth" the universe and all within it; God *is* the universe and all within it.

Of course, this perspective makes God not a "person" in the sense we might understand the term (that is, that God is a conscious, unique, and separate being with human characteristics and tendencies) but makes God, in effect, a "thing," comparable to gravity.

Unfortunately, such an idea can sound a bit insulting—at least to some people's way of thinking—but such an objection demonstrates a marked lack of understanding of Eastern concepts of divinity. The Eastern mind considers recognizing the Divine in all things to be the purest form of adoration or worship possible, while the Western insistence on making God personal (or human, for that matter) would be to minimize the Divine. In essence, to the Easterner the transcendent God of Western religion is insulting in that it presumes the Divine might be contained within the parameters of a single entity or being.

There is a sense in which worshipping an impersonal deity is problematic; after all, how does one form a relationship with what can best be described as a cosmic force or ubiquitous energy field of some kind? It really would be tantamount to worshipping the sun and, to some minds, about as rewarding.

This lack of a personal God often proves to be a huge stumbling block for some and one of the chief reasons the concept of an immanent God has been traditionally rejected by Westerners. Unfortunately, this is a result of failing to dig deeply enough into the subject to understand that even within an immanent deity, there is still room for a cosmic personality.

What the Westerner is railing against here is an ancient concept of God known as *pantheism*, a perception that holds God to be simply an impersonal force that permeates everything and gives it life. In fact, this force *is* life itself, broken down into its most basic elements, all of them existing eternally as part of a greater whole and, as such, not something that can be related to personally in any real sense. Such a concept of God, then, really is not much different from no belief in God, for the end results are essentially the same and equally irrelevant.

But there is another perception of God held to within Eastern thought that does allow for the existence of a type of divine personality, which is closer to what I am suggesting here. Known as *panentheism*, it is similar to pantheism in that it perceives everything as being a part of God, but panentheism also believes that this everything *includes all consciousness and thought.* The panentheist works from the premise that thought is a form of energy and assumes that if all energy exists as a single unit, it stands to reason that all conscious thought does so as well, forming a type of "collective" or universal consciousness we all tap into—either consciously or unconsciously—as a byproduct of our existence. In effect, it is this consciousness we label "God" that serves as the source from which the individual soul emerges.

Which concept one embraces becomes vitally important in understanding the nature of the soul as well as the rationale behind reincarnation. From the perspective of the transcendent God of Western theology, the soul is not a *part* of God, *but His creation*, much like the universe itself. At best, we may reflect this divine nature in some way, much as a painting will reflect the skills of the artist or a son reflect the personality of his father, but for the most part we are created beings separate from it. To the immanent God, however, the human soul is an emanation of itself—a molecule, if you will—of the greater consciousness that permeates all matter and energy throughout the universe. It is not something that God *creates* and then sends on its way, but something that God *is*. As such, a soul can be neither created nor destroyed any more than God Himself could be, for the one is an integral part of the other. In essence, just as the human body could not exist without each molecule that makes it up, so too God could not exist without each soul. They are inseparable.

The implications of this are profound, for since the universe itself is in a constant state of change, then God too must be constantly changing, making God, in effect, an evolving deity that uses reincarnation to realize this continual process of growth (in marked contrast to the unchanging, transcendent God of Western religion). Which position one gravitates toward concerning the nature of God, then, will go far in determining whether one can embrace reincarnation as a valid belief system or whether one must discard it as, at best, an unnecessary appendage to understanding the nature of reality. To the person who believes in a God that exists apart from and separate from His own creation, reincarnation seems wholly impractical—at least insofar as traditional Western religion is concerned—yet for the person who can imagine a God that is thoroughly integrated into the very essence of life itself, reincarnation is not only reasonable but almost a requirement. In fact, it would be difficult to imagine it not being a major part of the equation, when one considers the nature of immanent divinity carefully.

The Illusion of Separateness

However, if each of us is inherently a part of God, then why does God *seem* to be so separate from ourselves? Clearly, God appears to be interacting *with* His creation, not as if it were a *part* of Himself but as if He were external to it. As such, the argument might be made that the belief in the unity of all life is purely an illusion, and that in fact we are actually all unique and individual creations, each emanating from the same source, thus bringing the entire need for rebirth into serious question.

So how do we deal with this disparity? In fact, we don't, for the truth of the matter is that both perceptions are, in a way, correct. We *are* all a part of a much larger universal essence, yet we *perceive* ourselves—and God for that matter—as separate, because it is the very perception of separateness that provides us the opportunity to understand the all-encompassing nature of the Divine. The illusion of a God who exists "out there," then, is a necessary one we must maintain as a result of our limited ability to comprehend God in a way we can intellectually fathom. To reduce Him to terms as simple as possible, we must turn God into something considerably smaller than Himself—into little "bite-sized" pieces, if you will—because we aren't capable of digesting Him whole.

Unfortunately, this piecemeal approach to God often results in confusion and a multitude of contradictory and sometimes unsettling images of the Divine. For example, some people perceive God as kind and loving while others perceive him as angry, cruel, and judgmental. Yet how can He be both at the same time? Doesn't this tendency to want to craft God in our own image reduce our understanding of the Divine rather than enhance it?

To some degree, this is true; our understanding or "picture" of God is determined by our own level of spiritual maturity, which is why there are so many different "Gods" to choose from. We simply craft Him in *our* image and continue to do so until such a time as we might grow beyond the need for such images and move toward a more mature understanding of the Divine. But this is not entirely a bad thing, for in permitting us the luxury of crafting God in our image, it allows us to see the underlying sameness that permeates all images of the Divine that we maintain. This is not only to be expected, but could even be considered an important part of the process of understanding the vastness of the Divine, which truly can be all things to all people.

Yet simply because we are often unclear and even contradictory in our definition of God, that does not mean our perceptions are entirely wrong. The analogy of light is perfect for expressing this truth. If we were to perceive the full range of the spectrum of light in its entirety, it would appear as a single point of brilliant white light. There would be no reds or blues or greens, for when all the colors of the rainbow are merged together they appear as white. We have to break the white light down—through the prism we know as separateness—in order to make out the various colors of the spectrum, before we can perceive any single color. As such, even though red is but one part of the white light, once we can see it as a separate color we can then appreciate it as a unique element of the greater whole, and even compare it to all the other colors in the spectrum.

While recognizing that God is the sum of all, we must similarly break God down into smaller parts in order to perceive that truth. This is the reason for the multitude of religions on our planet; God is simply too big to be seen in His entirety, and thus our natural inclination is to personalize the Divine into something we can understand and comprehend. Enlightenment, then, is simply the ability to perceive the "light" in its totality and recognize that one can learn from any of the various hues or colors it has been broken down into. The colors are not truly illusions, for they do exist within the greater spectrum of light, but they are isolated so we can perceive them with our limited perspective. We need the illusion of separateness in order to have some context within which to understand unity and, with it, the Divine.

Recognizing Our Inherent Divinity

It may be overwhelming to consider that each of us is, in essence, divine, but without that realization reincarnation has no real point. We reincarnate in order to experience life in all its many facets so that the Divine within may experience life in all its many facets as well. This is not to diminish God by making His experiences dependent upon our own, but to enlarge God to encompass the vast range of human—and, no doubt, all sentient life—experience. Nor is it blasphemous to declare our own divinity, for to do so is simply to understand our source and purpose for being here. In fact, the danger to humanity lies in failing to embrace that reality and therefore diminishing the Divine in the process. It is when we consider ourselves separate from the Creator that we live in darkness. Recognizing our oneness with the source of all life—not as an artificial construct of the Divine but as a vibrant, living element of it—is what gives us the power to experience the love and joy that is God. Teach a person she is born a sinner apart from God, and she will live according to that belief; tell the same person that she is a child of the Divine, and she will invariably realize the light that lives within her. Anything less would be to dishonor the Divine and ourselves.

If it is necessary to perceive God as something separate from ourselves in order to comprehend any element of God's divinity, then it is an inevitable byproduct that each soul will also see itself as a separate and unique element apart from all other souls. And therein lies the great paradox Eastern mysticism speaks of: just as the need to imagine God as a separate thing from ourselves is necessary to truly begin to perceive God's completeness, so too do we individualized souls require the same illusion of separateness to experience what we are, both in essence and substance. In effect, while we are a part of each other, it is essential that we *forget that fact* if we are to experience anything on other than a purely conceptual basis.

It is this very illusion of separateness, then, that permits us—and, by extension, God—to differentiate what we call good from evil or right from wrong, or even left from right for that matter, for each can only be understood and experienced within the context of *what they are not*. Without the illusion of individuality to work from, good and evil—for example—could only be understood conceptually. But in order to experience the full range of existence—with all its infinite joys and sorrows—it cannot be merely conceived of intellectually, but must be realized practically. This is why we need separateness: we simply cannot experience anything without it.

And that is what the soul is and does. It is an individualized part of the Divine that exists purely to experience life in all its many facets. Who we are, then, is merely a reflection of what facet of Himself God wishes to experience. We are "spirit stuff" on an adventure; the Divine Spark on holiday setting out on that remarkable journey we call physicality or—more simply—life itself. That is the machine behind the process and the very point of reincarnation as well as the rationale behind every step we take and every path we choose to explore. It is God experiencing Himself through us—and as us—in the adventure of a lifetime or, in the case of reincarnation, many lifetimes.

chapter five
Soul versus Personality

So how does the soul accomplish this "knowing itself" from the spiritual realm? Even if we accept the idea that the soul is part of the greater godhood, that still doesn't tell us how it is able to experience all these different lifetimes from its side of eternity. Clearly, there must be some sort of mechanism that allows it to enter into physicality, whereby it might experience things firsthand—to come to "know itself," so to speak, by entering into a realm in which it experiences itself in a context outside of its own inherent divinity.

It does this by generating what we call an ego, or personality, which is that part of ourselves we think of as uniquely and distinctly "us." In other words, think of the soul as a type of "ego factory" that is constantly generating completely new and different personalities, each of which it uses to experience the limitations made possible only by coming "into the flesh."

This can get confusing, however, if we fail to make the distinction between these two aspects of ourselves. As such, it might prove helpful to define more carefully precisely what a personality is and how it differs from the soul. In other words, just where does the "soul" end and the "personality" begin and, even more importantly, how do we differentiate between the two?

For the most part, we tend to think of the soul and the personality—which Freud referred to as the ego—as interchangeable terms, yet that is where the confusion starts. The soul and the personality are *not* the same thing. Although the personality is a reflection of the soul that animates it, the soul is more than merely another term for the personality.

It is the personality that gives the soul the ability to experience life within the physical realm of time and space. Without a manifest personality, the soul is unable to interact with the world, for the physical plane of existence is foreign to it. In a way, then, the personality is like a diving suit that permits the swimmer to descend deep beneath the water without being crushed or drowned, a feat that would be impossible without such a device. In effect, the soul simply can't manifest itself on our plane of existence without an "ego suit" within which to roam about.

Perhaps the best analogy is that of a light bulb. In and of itself, the light bulb is a fairly useless and quite fragile object. By the same token, electricity in and of itself is not very useful (and, in fact, is even dangerous and potentially destructive). However, once the two elements are brought together—once the bulb is plugged into a socket and energized by electricity—they both become very useful items indeed. Despite the fact that neither has much in common (one being entirely physical and the other existing as pure energy), when combined they form a perfect merging of matter and energy. In effect, in order for either the electricity or the light bulb to be of any practical use, they need each other.

The soul and the personality work in much the same way: the soul is part of the divine current that courses through the universe, powering everything; the personality is that which the soul energizes. The difference between the soul and the personality versus electricity and the light bulb, however, is that unlike electricity, the soul is a conscious entity (in fact, it *is* consciousness itself), while the personality is, unlike the light bulb, immortal. Even though it appears the light bulb has a very short life span from the perspective of linear time, both it and the electricity that powers it exist forever from the perspective of eternity. It is all simply a matter of one's point of view.

In effect, then, the personality is a manifestation of the soul that generates it, making it to some degree a reflection of its "parent" soul. Another way to think of it might be to understand the soul as a type of template from which each personality is generated. However, unlike a basic blueprint of a home, which might be used to build hundreds of identical dwellings, each personality impacts and subtly changes the template or blueprint itself—which then generates the next personality with these modifications in mind. In other words, each personality is a "snapshot" that demonstrates where on its spiritual journey the soul is or, more precisely, reflects its level of spiritual maturity in much the same way that a thermometer measures the ambient temperature of the room one is in.

What is important to recognize is that the soul empowers the personality, and the personality then becomes a reflection of the soul that is animating it. The two aspects work hand in hand to form a complete and total life experience—either positive or negative—in a symbiotic and mutually beneficial dance of life. As such, whatever exists within the furthest reaches of the soul—be it love, kindness, and compassion or the more base elements of human nature, such as hatred, cruelty, and indifference—will be reflected by the personality the soul generates.

Of course, one might ask the question of how—if the soul is a part of the greater divine soul and, as such, presumably a thing of light and love—it can manifest the occasional negative, or "wicked," personality. In other words, if our personality is a reflection of our soul's level of spiritual maturity and our soul is a part of God, how can we be anything other than what God inherently is? Where would traits such as anger, ambition, lust, greed, or hatred come from if our personality is simply reflecting the soul within us, and that soul is reflecting the inherent nature of divinity itself?

The answer is that while the fundamental nature of all souls is one of love and light, in younger souls[8] that nature can be suppressed and, indeed, *must* be suppressed, for the fullest range of human experiences to be realized. In other words, a soul might intentionally move into darkness simply to experience what darkness is, and thus manifest a "dark" personality as a result. Even in that case, however, the soul is still inherently a thing of love, but one that has purposely *chosen* to forget that fact so that it may have a wider range of experiences, as well as more fully interact with other souls in its journey.

This is not to suggest, however, that a young soul is synonymous with an evil soul (which does not exist in any case). To be a young soul simply means to be innocent or even, to some degree, naïve. However, just as naïve people can often be easily persuaded to engage in bad behavior purely as a result of their not knowing better, so too might a young soul generate a personality that lacks the wisdom acquired through many lifetimes to overcome the negativity or disadvantages of being born into a particularly violent environment or by being raised in a dysfunctional setting. By way of an example, the soul that generated Adolf Hitler was not evil, but the personality it generated did great evil as a result of being born into the family, culture, and time that it was.

But who, then, is really calling the shots, so to speak, in life—the personality or the soul?

It is the personality—that which we call the ego—that dominates within the physical realm and makes the decisions about what it will experience or not experience within the context of any given incarnation. This is essential, for if the soul were in charge, it would always operate in perfect accordance with its divine nature and so never be able to "know itself" because it would live exclusively in the light all

---

8. We will examine the issue of soul "age" in more detail later.

the time. It is the ability to live in darkness afforded by the personality that permits the soul to understand what "light" even means.

What is interesting about this is that, although it is the personality that is directly interacting within the physical realm, it is the soul that is being most impacted by every event, experience, and person that comes into its frame of reference. It is shaped by the culmination of a lifetime of experiences and a host of environmental factors that all align themselves to determine the soul's adventures as well as define its personality "type" while in this incarnation.

However, the resultant personality, while influenced by environmental factors and personal experiences, does not depart from the primary characteristics of the soul that energizes it. In other words, a more mature or seasoned soul—in being closer in nature to its divine source and thus less prone to violence—will remain peaceful, despite whatever negative environmental factors it may encounter in any given manifestation. This is why people born into a particularly violent culture may choose not to participate in the brutality and may even make attempts to change the violent nature of the world they find themselves thrust into (often suffering martyrdom for their efforts in the process). In fact, such people are often the catalysts for great change in their society, even if they use violence in the process. John Brown's raid at Harpers Ferry in 1859 is a good example of an advanced soul resorting to violence to effect social change—in this case, the elimination of slavery—and dying in the effort.[9]

In essence, then, there is no such thing as a "good" or a "bad" soul. There are only souls that have come a long way in their journey and souls that have just started out, and the personalities they generate will be shaped by the degree of understanding they possess up to that

9. John Brown (1800–59) was an ardent abolitionist who frequently used violence in his attempts to bring an end to slavery. In a naïve and futile effort to end slavery in the South, his raid on a federal armory at Harpers Ferry, Virginia (now West Virginia), in October of 1859, was designed as a means by which he might arm thousands of slaves. The rebellion was quickly suppressed by federal forces, and Brown was tried and hanged several weeks later.

point. It's the experiences of life that shape the personality and determine whether one is good or bad, while the soul that empowers isn't capable of being either.

Does the Personality Die?

But what, then, becomes of the personality—the "recording device" of the soul—upon death? Does the soul, as is widely believed, separate from the personality and move on while the personality, like the body within which it was encased, is discarded, destroying a lifetime of memories in the process?

Western religion sees the personality living on eternally in an unchanging and unchangeable state, while Eastern religion—and reincarnationists—maintain that they are not only separate elements of ourselves but that these elements separate upon death, with the soul manifesting another entirely fresh and unique personality and the old personality falling by the wayside. This is thought to be necessary since the external personality—being largely artificial and contrived in any case—can often impede spiritual growth. As such, so that the soul may mature, it—like a butterfly that has outgrown its need for its cocoon—is left behind in order for the soul to be truly set free. To retain the shed personality would not only hinder that process dramatically, but would keep us living in a past that no longer exists in linear time. As such, all memories of a past life must be purged from our present consciousness in order for the process to proceed, and that past can't be truly purged as long as the shed personality remains intact. Unfortunately, this suggests that, by declaring the personality (or ego) to be a temporal aspect of a soul to be discarded upon death while the soul continues on to its next incarnation, all experiences of an entire lifetime are eternally lost. The personality must live on in some capacity in order for the soul to maintain the life lessons that personality experienced, but how can it exist once it is separated from the soul?

There are two possibilities to consider. The first is what's known as the "feeder soul" concept, and the second is called the "repeater soul" concept. In the feeder soul concept, the soul is distinctly separate from the various personalities that emanate from it. In other words, while the single soul may produce countless personalities that incarnate into the flesh, it is larger than any single one of them and is, in fact, far more expansive than we can begin to appreciate. One soul may generate many personalities though no single personality is the complete reflection of the larger, underlying soul. In other words, the soul is the source or "feed" for all the various personalities that emanate from it, without being uniquely identified with any one of them. In this concept, then, the soul is our spiritual "parent" that births us, and each of our previous and future personalities are our spiritual "siblings."

A good analogy would be that of a tree that is constantly putting out a thick outcropping of leaves, each of which represents an individual human personality. Just as with a regular tree, where the leaves serve the purpose of providing the tree with the much-needed photosynthesis it requires to grow, so too does each personality provide the soul with the life experiences it needs to grow. The "leaves" of each personality may eventually be shed, but the experiences each provided went into enhancing and maturing the "tree" of the soul itself. Even if the individual personality no longer exists, the essence of what it was and what it experienced during its brief sojourn on Earth remains an integral part of the tree.

Another way to imagine this is to see the soul as a library and all the individual books on its shelves the cumulative knowledge acquired by hundreds of personalities over the ages. As each new personality is introduced into the realm of the physical universe, it "writes" another book that is eventually stored in the main library and will always remain there, long after the original author is dead. Therefore, the complete essence of what that personality was remains eternally inscribed within the pages of the countless volumes lining each shelf, and in that sense it exists forever.

But what becomes of each of our past-life personas once the soul that generates them all finishes its rebirthing cycle? If all human personalities exist within the single moment of "now" with regard to the spiritual realm, each of our past personalities should effectively "bump" into each other and even interact in some ways. If this is the case, however, is it possible all these personalities could be ultimately integrated into a complete and utterly astonishing "superego" made up of literally hundreds or thousands of personalities? Imagine suddenly remembering everyone you ever knew throughout the course of a thousand lifetimes, or every thought, experience, and scrap of knowledge acquired over twenty thousand years—purified and sanctified—and now subject to instant recall with no more difficulty than it takes to recall one's current phone number. The possibilities stagger the imagination.

The other theory, the "repeater soul" concept, works from the premise that the soul and personality do not separate at all, but each personality becomes an embedded "memory" of the soul itself. In other words, unlike the feeder soul concept, the repeater soul does not simply reproduce various personalities and send them to experience physicality, but instead it experiences the physical realm personally and individually. In this way, then, we remain essentially the same person through each of our incarnations, even though we may reincarnate into a different gender or race. As such, if your inner person is essentially a giving and compassionate one, that would manifest or imprint itself onto each succeeding personality, making it possible that you reincarnate with a similar personality each time (though a part of that would be determined by environment and experiences). In essence, you may not be all that different a person in your next incarnation than you are in this one. Older and wiser, it is hoped, but essentially still the same person.

This concept corresponds more closely to the analogy of an actor who takes on many roles, learning and growing with each new part he plays. While the soul/actor may start out uncertain, as it takes on more "roles" (that is, incarnations), it grows in skill and experience until eventually it becomes a formidable performer, filled with wisdom and talent. In the same way, we change roles throughout our lifetime—from infant to child to adolescent to adult to spouse to parent, and so on—so too does each role come and go and, while the individual roles and most of the lines that were spoken have long since been forgotten (or, more correctly, cast off), the actor behind the roles continues to live on.

Just as we are no longer the person we were thirty, twenty, ten, or even five years ago, so too does the soul change as it moves on to new and ever more challenging parts, leaving the old roles—as instructive as they may have been—in the past. It is a thoroughly forward-looking soul that is seeking only to grow ever closer to the Divine, and sees each role it plays in that process as stepping stones along the way.

The problem with the repeater soul concept, however, is that it elicits confusion. For example, if I was John in eighteenth-century England, Sasha in nineteenth-century Russia, and Carl in twentieth-century America, which is the *real* me? In the feeder soul concept, they would all be unrelated expressions of the real soul that I am, but with the repeater concept they are all related expressions of myself that, in effect, supersede each other. In other words, with each new incarnation I reinvent myself, effectively erasing the old "chalkboard" that contained my previous life and writing a new life afresh on the recently erased surface. As such, John, Sasha, and Carl no longer exist except within my soul's memory, and even then they can only be accessed through hypnosis.

Conclusions

I don't know if this has been more useful than confusing, but no one ever said the mechanics of reincarnation are simple—only that they are useful to understanding the nature of reality. Which notion the reader finds more personally helpful is, of course, a matter of preference. I personally believe the repeater soul concept more closely corresponds to what we see played out in regression therapy, for the current personality seems much more likely to be affected—either negatively or positively—by a previous personality only if they are one and the same. With the feeder soul concept I find it more difficult to explain how a trauma that impacts one personality would easily be transferred onto another entirely separate personality. While it makes sense that the feeder soul might well acquire experience and knowledge from many personalities and then shape the next incarnation from these experiences, it seems to me one would be suffering from numerous traumas experienced by multiple past-life personas, whereas most past-life traumas seem to find their source in only a single past-life personality. However, this may only be a limitation of my understanding, and so I will not insist on either concept being the "correct" one. Nor would I be surprised if, in some strange way, both concepts were true to some degree, especially as we're dealing with that which takes place outside the venue of linear time and space and within the mysterious world—from our perspective—of the spiritual realm.

chapter six

Echoes

In an effort to better illustrate how past-life experiences may influence our present life in both subtle and significant ways, I present this story of a man whose life may have been heavily affected by just such a past experience—an "echo," if you will, of another life lived in another time that still somehow managed to influence and even dramatically impact his adolescence.

I know the person behind this story well, and I can assure you he is not particularly anxious to share it with the reading public, yet he feels it is necessary to do so for the sake of clarification. The subject recounts these experiences and observations only after great internal debate and no small amount of trepidation, but believes it so important in illustrating how reincarnation might work in the daily lives of ordinary people that he is willing to put himself under the glare of the harsh lights of scrutiny and, quite likely, subject himself to some degree of ridicule. Yet sometimes personal privacy must be sacrificed upon the altar of knowledge in order that learning might take place.

The man I speak of here is, of course, myself. The events I'm about to relate are true insofar as I remember them accurately, and I will endeavor to present them as objectively and dispassionately as I am capable of doing. I realize many will simply dismiss them as adolescent fantasies or, at best, unusual coincidences, and I make no claims to the contrary. I will only present what happened to me in a straight-forward manner and let you, the reader, decide for yourself whether my experience has anything to say to you on a personal level.

———

My story begins around the time of my twelfth birthday. Up to then I had been a rather ordinary boy growing up in a large Catholic family on a farm near St. Cloud, Minnesota. I was not an unusual child in any way—perhaps a bit more precocious than most and certainly imaginative—but from all outward appearances I was a typical product of the American Midwest, and while my parents had a difficult marriage, for the most part I remember my childhood as being relatively carefree.

My parents divorced a year before my eleventh birthday, and my siblings and I had just moved with my stepfather to Colorado when things began to change. Whereas previously my interests had been rather conventional—tending toward stereotypical male interests such as dinosaurs, racing cars, and toy trucks—as I approached adolescence I began developing an unusual fascination with things having to do with the military. Where I got my newfound interest was unknown, for my family did not possess any significant military background, and so there seemed no obvious external influences that might have triggered my new interest. And yet as I moved into my teen years, my fascination for all things military—from toy soldiers and plastic tanks to war movies on television—grew exponentially.

Eventually most of my reading material dealt with military history—specifically the Second World War—and, not surprisingly, once I became a competent model builder, my bedroom became a virtual museum of aircraft, tanks, and ship models. Moreover, once I acquired the financial resources I also began accumulating a considerable collection of bayonets, helmets, shoulder patches, and even a few World War II–era rifles and pistol duplicates. One could say I was a military "nut" bordering on the obsessed, and while it's not that I didn't have other interests as well, they paled in comparison to the time and energy—and money—I put into my fascination with the military. In fact, it is fair to say that for the most part, the military in general and World War II in particular *were* my life at the time or, at least, a big part of it.

More than that, as I moved further into adolescence I found myself increasingly sliding into a largely imaginary world in which I fantasized about being a soldier in combat. Always something of a loner, I would spend hours in the forests surrounding my home fighting fantasy battles using a steel rod as a rifle. These fantasy battles grew increasingly elaborate and complex in detail each time I played them out until it got to the point where I could almost visualize the gruesome carnage in my mind's eye. Additionally, my imaginary battles were remarkably similar in both scope and depth: I invariably imagined myself an infantryman battling an influx of enemy tanks in a forest. The script never varied, and I seemingly never tired of my unchanging role in the drama, as though it were a play I had performed a hundred times before.

My fascination for the military also manifested itself in other ways as well. At thirteen I joined a local chapter of the Civil Air Patrol (CAP), a paramilitary Air Force auxiliary, which gave me the opportunity to wear oversized Air Force uniforms and march about like a soldier for hours at a time. I genuinely enjoyed the military atmosphere the CAP exposed me to, from drills to moving up through the ranks. I even had the opportunity to spend a week at the Air Force Academy, near Colorado Springs, one summer, an experience that gave me my first real taste of military life, and one that set my immediate path for me. It was inevitable, then, that I would eventually find my way into the armed forces after high school, enlisting in the U.S. Navy immediately after graduating. I seemed "born" to be a military man, and as such found the discipline and drilling of basic training much easier to endure than many of my shipmates did.

This obsession stayed with me for the next few years, only beginning to wane slowly once I left the military and got married. Even then, however, it didn't dissipate completely, but continued to follow me even into art school, where many of my drawings had a decidedly military theme to them. Fortunately, however, by the time I entered my thirties, much of the allure I had previously felt at last began to fade as I made a concerted effort to expand my areas of interest. Today, while I still maintain an interest in military history and enjoy military-themed movies, I no longer retain my fixation with all things military. Though I still own a few books on the subject, most simply sit on a shelf collecting dust, and while I still occasionally find myself watching a History Channel feature on the Second World War, it no longer holds me captive as it once did. I have outgrown my earlier obsession and consider myself more of a peacemaker than the warmonger I once was. In fact, I now look back upon my childhood fascination with a mixture of curiosity and embarrassment, and wonder to this day what might have triggered such a unique adolescence.

A Question of Environment

So where did my fascination with all things military come from—in particular, my obsession with World War II?

Again, I did not come from a military family. My birth father was a factory worker; my stepfather, the manager of a local Elks Club. Although I had the usual mix of male relatives who were World War II veterans, their experiences were never recounted (at least around me) nor were they important to our family's dynamics. In my home, the war—meaning World War II—rarely came up as a topic of conversation, and if it did it was in hushed tones, as though it were something to be fervently forgotten. As such, it is clear that I can't blame my obsession on a steady diet of war stories told to an impressionable boy by a phalanx of battle-tested uncles.

Television? Certainly that was an influence. The era I grew up in was the golden age of such war-themed television programs as *McHale's Navy*, *Hogan's Heroes*, and *Rat Patrol*, and movies like *The Longest Day* and *Twelve O'Clock High* were popular fare at the time. But did these programs trigger within me an unusual interest in military history, or did I naturally gravitate toward such programs because of an already inherent interest in the military? In other words, did the shows I watch instill within me a military obsession, or did I watch such programs because they fed into the military obsession I already possessed? Undoubtedly these programs enhanced—and, perhaps, even helped define—my growing preoccupation, but what was it about war-themed entertainment that so attracted me in the first place, especially considering my non-military upbringing? And, further, why *only* the Second World War? I showed no similar interest in the First World War, the Civil War, Vietnam, or other American or foreign conflicts. Why this particular conflict only?

As I look back over my life, I recall other idiosyncrasies I developed during this time as well. Perhaps the most curious of these was a penchant for only one type of footwear: black Wellington boots. I never cared for athletic footwear or hiking boots (though either might have made more sense considering the amount of hiking I did). Why Wellingtons, which are far from the most comfortable or practical shoes available?

Students of military history, however, might find my footwear fetish interesting. Boots very similar to what we now refer to as "Wellingtons" were standard issue for German soldiers during the Second World War. They were known as "jackboots" and were to eventually become as synonymous with the German army of World War II as that army's distinctive low-rimmed helmet. Had I developed a preference for such impractical footwear in a vacuum, or were those boots already unconsciously familiar to me by virtue of having worn them in some long-forgotten past?

There were other signals as well: the only foreign language I ever took an interest in while in high school was German, and though I never became particularly proficient at it, I enjoyed learning what little of the language I did. I especially enjoyed listening to the instructors from Austria and Germany who taught these courses, finding their musings about their homes as interesting as learning the language itself. I had an almost insatiable interest in their countries and felt I would be comfortable living there, though I had no particularly compelling reason why I should feel that way.

Finally, another curious interest of mine at the time was dirigibles, those massive lighter-than-air vessels that floated majestically through the skies between the world wars. By the time I was sixteen I had already become something of an expert on them and spent many hours drawing pictures of the great airships. Was it a mere coincidence that most of these vessels were of German manufacture? And, again, where did this particular interest derive from? There certainly was nothing in my immediate environment (or, for that matter, on television) to have triggered such a fascination.

Putting the Clues Together

So what are we to make of all this? Why the fascination with a war that had ended more than a decade before I was born? Why the preoccupation with all things military in a boy who had no contact with the real world of the military, and why the preference for black Wellington boots, the affinity for German, and the intense interest in airships?

In and of themselves, none of these interests would appear to be particularly significant, but together they seemed to be pointing me toward something. There was a unifying theme to them all, and it all had to do with Germany and the Second World War (or, in the case of the airships, the immediate prewar years). But what did it all mean?

Environment does little to account for these obsessions. My five siblings showed no similar affinities despite comparable family backgrounds. Only I had these interests—proclivities that eventually proved to be a source of embarrassment to me while managing to remain strangely natural at the same time. Something was drawing me to these interests—something outside the realm of my normal daily experiences or cultural inclinations. I assumed they meant I was simply odd, but I wonder . . . could they have been more than inexplicable eccentricities? Could they have been, in fact, nothing less than snippets of a past life— "echoes," if you will, of a previous incarnation that were still resonating within my life?

I have no conscious memories of having been in a World War II infantry/armored battle of the kind I described earlier, but is it possible I had been, and had somehow retained those "memories" in the deepest recesses of my subconscious? Certainly such battles as I imagined were quite common in Russia throughout much of World War II. Was it merely a coincidence that Hitler's drive into Russia in the summer of 1941 was a favorite historical theme for me, and the one element of the entire war that seemed most poignant?

Or were these elements nothing more than—as the rationalist would maintain—the product of an overactive imagination, perhaps enhanced by a sense of isolation and a lack of maturity? No doubt psychiatrists could offer a purely natural rationale to explain my unusual past: it was just the way my brain is "wired" or perhaps I was a far more suggestible child upon whom television had a more profound impact than even I realized.

I suppose there are other possible explanations to explain my experiences, but none of them seem to add up. My affinities were too specific, too consistent, too theme-oriented to be mere boyhood fantasies. Background, environmental influences, television—none of these answer the question of why there was an extremely limited and frequently Germanic theme to my interests. If it were all a product of media, shouldn't my interests have been all over the board, so to speak, with little correlation or consistency to them? Shouldn't they have likewise extended to other conflicts as well, such as the American Civil War or even some of the great wars of antiquity?

The possibility that I was unconsciously recounting a past memory—diluted and incomplete as it was—never occurred to me until many years later. It wasn't until I began examining the concept of reincarnation that the possibility I had actually lived another lifetime—perhaps as a German soldier in World War II—became a distinct possibility. That possibility seemed to explain the "imaginary" tank battles, my affinity for black Wellington boots and the German language, and my fascination with World War II far more thoroughly and with far less complexity than traditional psychological explanations.

But how, if such were the case, did it work? I can only offer conjecture here, but I suspect in it there may be more than a tiny seed of truth.

For the sake of argument, let us suppose for a moment I had been a young man born in Germany before the Second World War who not only took great pride in his country but went on to serve as a soldier in that conflict. Further, imagine I had fought a desperate battle in the forests of Russia, and that battle cost me my life. And, finally, let's say the soul of that young man, after a brief sojourn in limbo (or wherever it is disembodied souls may loiter), entered the developing fetus of a Minnesota woman in 1957.

What would be the potential consequences of such a transfer? Could the young soldier's death have been so traumatic that even the process of rebirth could not entirely obliterate the deep scars it left on his psyche and thus he carried them into this newest incarnation—not as a consciously recalled memory, but as an impression that influenced him in subtle and inexplicable ways? Could it have ultimately manifested itself in this preoccupation with the circumstances surrounding this young man's death—the most horrific war known to humanity—as well as left vague memories of a language he had spoken long ago but had since forgotten, and even a preference for a type of footwear he wore every day in his forgotten march across Russia? And wouldn't my interest in dirigibles perfectly mirror those of a German boy growing up in the 1930s who had personally seen the great airships of his day glide gracefully across the sky (and who would have been approximately the same age as I was when I first developed such an interest)?

I call these "echoes" from the past, not memories. Memories are specific and data driven; echoes are more akin to impressions or inexplicable affections, interests, likes, and dislikes one develops almost spontaneously that shape our nature in subtle ways we are often entirely unaware of. One needn't even believe in reincarnation for them to shape one's persona; the process goes on regardless of, and often in spite of, our beliefs. It is the nature of the soul, and it is relentless.

But why would such residual interests and fascinations remain? What purpose, if any, might they serve? Who knows? Perhaps my earlier preoccupation was an important element in my spiritual development. Perhaps in order to evolve into a man of peace, it was required I understand the horrors of war—an understanding that might have been impossible without some of my former incarnation's experiences being imprinted upon my new psyche. Then again, it may just simply be a flaw in the rebirth process—I don't know.

In any case, I am firmly convinced that what happened to me has happened to—and continues to happen to—literally millions of people around the world. Many quite normal people claim feelings of familiarity—a sense of déjà vu—about places and events from the past, and while some and, perhaps, even most, may well be purely imaginary, can *all* of them be explained away so easily? I had an active imagination as a boy (just as I still do today) but so do millions of other children, most of whom do not end up preoccupied with such a narrow range of interests for so many years. As such, the mystery for me remains unanswered and, perhaps, unanswerable.

Conclusions

So what is the reader to make of this story? I doubt if it changed any minds about reincarnation: there are enough curious elements in it for it to reinforce the concept of multiple births in those already persuaded of reincarnation's validity, and yet it lacks the kind of specifics or verifiable facts that might be of interest to the skeptic.

In spite of this, I believe I am not alone in these feelings of having lived another life. I am convinced many people have found their personal histories shaped by interests and infatuations outside the scope of what might be expected. In fact, if reincarnation were a fact, shouldn't we almost *expect* such experiences to manifest themselves in our current lives as they seem to have done in mine? I leave it to my readers to decide that for themselves.

chapter seven

A Tale of Two Worlds

Reincarnation cannot be understood without first making some decisions concerning the nature of the universe itself. While it is possible to move through the process of spiritual maturation without a clear understanding of how the universe is actually constructed (just as it's possible to be an excellent driver without having a clue as to how a combustion engine works), it is equally true that once one understands the nature of time and space, the entire process becomes a little easier to fathom. Only then can reincarnation be appreciated for the intricate and complex machine it is, for it is nothing less than the road map to immortality.

While it may appear presumptuous to assume one can reduce the cosmos to an easily understood equation, it is still helpful to consider some possibilities, if only in an effort to develop a basis from which to work. Just as mountain climbers work their way upward through a series of pre-established camps on their way to the summit, it is likewise essential that we construct a "base camp" from which to start our journey if we hope to make more than a halfhearted thrust for the top. While, admittedly, my camp may not be entirely adequate to meet all our needs, it is still better than being trapped out in the barren and windswept open with nothing to guide us. As such, what I write here will be, by necessity, partially speculative and largely theoretical, and quite possibly entirely erroneous. I believe it is, however, at least internally consistent with what we understand of the process of reincarnation and, therefore, somewhere from which to begin our study.

The first thing that is important to examine is how we—especially in the West—understand the nature of reality (outside of a purely materialistic sense) and, specifically, how we perceive the realm of the spirit.

Most of us understand life to exist on two separate planes—the supernatural and the natural or, if you prefer, the world of spirit and the world of the flesh. These two realms are, from most people's perspective, separate and impassable, like two great continents divided by such a vast body of water that any attempt to bridge them must be, by necessity, one-way only. Additionally, it is generally taught that the one—the world of physicality within which we reside—is a largely artificial construct that was produced or created from within the realm of the spiritual world. In other words, the spiritual realm existed prior to the physical, with the latter being the byproduct of the creative energies of the former.

However, it is a myth that the spiritual realm and the physical realm are separate. They are, instead, intricately interwoven aspects of the same thing—namely, existence. In other words, there is no "spiritual" world that exists alongside the "physical" world; both are a part of a single reality—which we might call collectively the "natural" realm. Neither is a construct of the other, nor are they genuinely opposites of each other. They are more like two sides of the same coin that coexist eternally.

Dueling Cosmologies

Yet how is this possible? Doesn't logic itself tell us that the physical world must have had a beginning, just as it must ultimately have an end as well? After all, astronomy has shown us that the universe itself came into existence almost fourteen billion years ago with the Big Bang and that it will eventually come to end one day when all the usable energy of the cosmos is finally rendered inert. Therefore, if the very universe we live in is apparently a finite thing, why wouldn't we imagine that the physical world within which it exists would not also have a beginning and an end?

While this concept is certainly the norm among Westerners, it is a largely foreign concept to the Eastern mindset. In Eastern thought, the physical universe is incapable of being either created or destroyed and, as a result, has always existed and will always exist. While they may acknowledge that our universe is expanding outward at an increasing rate of speed, Easterners do not see that as being synonymous with entropy or ultimate extinction. Instead, they believe the universe to be cyclical—that is, that it expands and contracts in cycles, much like the beating of a heart. Many imagine that at some point— perhaps hundreds of billions of years from now—the outward expansion of the universe will cease and the entire thing will begin to slowly collapse back upon itself, eventually ending up where it started: as a single point of energy no larger than the head of a pin, suspended in a vast sea of nothingness, containing all the energy and mass of the universe. At that point—perhaps several hundred billions of years from now—the unimaginable gravitational forces contained within this single point of energy will become so great that it will have no choice but to explode, starting the entire process over again.

The problem is that we are looking at this process from a very limited perspective. We can see back to the birth of the universe 13.7 billion years ago, but when we do we generally assume that there was nothing that preceded that moment. As such, we perceive the universe to have had a "beginning" and thus naturally assume that, since we can measure the rate of expansion between the galaxies and see that they are moving ever farther apart from each other, that it will eventually have an "end" as well. We can't see that we may actually be only looking at a single beat of the celestial heart, never for a moment comprehending the truly eternal nature of it.

So which is it? Do we live in a constant-state universe—one that explodes, expands, and finally dies out, or could we be living in a cyclical universe that explodes, expands, contracts, and then repeats the process not twice or three times or even a hundred times, but forever?

Science doesn't accept the idea of a cyclical universe, mainly because we have not yet detected any mysterious force by which the universe might be induced to cease its outward expansion and begin contracting—but that is more an indictment of science's limitations than evidence that it is not so. In essence, we are still largely in our infancy with regard to understanding the nature of energy, time, and space. We simply haven't acquired enough data about our universe nor had the opportunity to explore it in all its glory, so the jury is still out—so to speak—when it comes to which is the more elegant model of our universe. However, it must be acknowledged that the cyclical-universe model does have the advantage of not having to account for how all the energy in the universe got here in the first place. It simply maintains that it has always been here and always will be here—in one form or another—throughout eternity (and thereby remaining consistent to the first law of thermodynamics, which tells us that energy can be neither created nor destroyed). There may be vast eons of time when the universe will be largely unusable as a stage upon which to allow souls to play out their sentient dramas, but eternity does not care if it takes five million or five billion years to form the first livable planets from the dust of an interstellar blast of energy. Creation will wait patiently, because it has all the time in the universe at its disposal.

While I don't wish to belabor the point, it is entirely possible that we live in an eternal universe, making it every bit as "old" as the spiritual realm it reflects. And this makes sense from the standpoint of logic as well, for what does it mean to have a spiritual realm if there is not also a physical realm to differentiate it? Without the one, the other is meaningless. Just as the color red becomes meaningless in a world in which everything is red, it is the existence of other colors that allows for there being anything we would call color at all. As such, there can be no "spiritual" realm if there is not also a "physical" realm, for the two are but opposite sides of the same coin. And just as one side of a coin cannot preexist the other, neither could one realm preexist the other. Either both are eternal or neither are, and if the latter, one has the difficult task of determining how either realm then came into being. Nothingness makes poor material from which to produce everything.

Two Worlds Coexisting as One

This doesn't mean the two worlds are mirror images of each other, however. They each operate by different laws—the physical universe within the context of linear time and space and the spiritual realm apart from it. In fact, it is this difference that makes the one world indispensable to the other. Without a physical universe of set laws that operate within the context of time and space, spirit cannot know anything experientially; and yet human consciousness cannot know immortality without the presence of a universe that exists without a clock. The one is essential for the other to be realized, giving each a codependent, symbiotic relationship. This allows us, once we grasp this principle, to understand that the two worlds are not separate but instead exist as a single unit. They are also constantly interacting with one another, spirit moving into the physical realm and the physical moving back into the world of pure spirit, in an unending cycle of pure experience.

If we accept the notion that souls reincarnate, we can see this interaction between the two realms played out very clearly. A soul, seeking to experience things on a level other than the purely theoretical, moves from one realm into the other and enters into a newborn child. At almost the same exact moment, an old man halfway around the world takes his final breath, and his spirit, freed now from the limitations of the physical realm, wings its way back toward the total freedom of spirit.

One enters just as another exits, much like a kind of eternally spinning turnstile.

To visualize this better, imagine a subway car coming to a stop at a station. As soon as the doors open, scores of people disembark while another two dozen people who had been waiting patiently on the platform step onboard. Hundreds still on the train do not move but simply remain seated, patiently waiting for their stop farther down the line. And thus the train moves on eternally, constantly dropping passengers off and picking up new ones, making a massive circuit around the city, forever.

The train, of course, represents our physical world of time and space, to which we are all subject as long as we remain onboard. The station is the spiritual realm from which we came and where we will eventually and repeatedly return. Therefore, both the train and the station serve vital functions in the never-ending cycle of existence.

This analogy implies that there's not much that separates the two realms and, indeed, that would be correct. The only thing that prevents us from seeing the other realm is our inability to perceive things that exist outside our physical senses. In effect, we sit within subway cars with smoked-glass windows that make it impossible to see either the embarking or departing passengers clearly (if at all), while those on the platform can peer into the interiors of the trains only with great difficulty. Those sitting inside the train and those standing outside on the platform may catch glimpses of the other, but it is not clear what they are seeing. Some might have better vision than others, and on occasion a few of the passengers and some of those standing on the platform manage to communicate, but for the most part they have only minimal contact with each other, which is as one would expect. After all, the embarking passengers, once they are onboard, have no real reason to keep in touch with those on the platform, while those disembarking have places to go and things to do; keeping in touch with those left behind on the train is not high on their list of priorities. Besides, both those embarking and those disembarking know they will run into each other down the line again (and perhaps even decide to ride together for a time).

So, what does all this mean in terms of our spiritual journey?

It means that ours really is a journey in the truest sense of the word, and once we realize it we can finally begin to relax, for at last we know what's happening. Too many people approach their own deaths terrified of what it will mean if they have to leave the train, uncertain of what they'll encounter once they step onto the platform and watch the train pull out of the station. Will they be assaulted in the dark, shadowy confines of some deserted waiting area? Will they get lost and stumble about for an eternity looking for someone to help them? Will there be anyone there to meet them as they had hoped, people who know the area and are prepared to help them find their way around? For people who have spent years riding the train and have no memory of having embarked on the journey, it can seem frightening to leave the train's familiar surroundings. Yet spiritually evolved individuals, as the seasoned travelers they are, know there's nothing to be afraid of. They understand the purpose of the train and know when it's time to get off. They see it not as a place of security (for, indeed, the train is the more dangerous place to be) but as a simple mode of transportation designed to take them from point A to point B. And, because of this knowledge, they can at last begin to enjoy the ride.

This analogy, however, while helping us begin to understand how the two worlds operate together, does not by any means cover the entire concept. What's not clear is how much one world might directly influence the other. It also doesn't touch upon the idea that there may be numerous "trains" running on many different tracks on journeys to an infinite number of stations, or whether it's possible for two of the trains to collide (and what that would mean for those onboard if they did). Further, my example makes it sound as though the train is moving along at a steady rate of speed, but the reality is that what we perceive as progression may in fact be nothing of the kind. The train is simply moving—not through time, but through an interdimensional matrix toward an infinite number of potential destinations along an infinite number of routes.

Conclusions

If all of this begins to get a little confusing and unnecessarily obtuse, it is better to leave it alone. It is only necessary to understand that everything that exists, be it in the physical realm or the spiritual, is intimately interconnected and interdependent upon the other realm for its existence and function. Only in understanding that does our purpose in constantly entering and leaving the physical plane make sense or serve any apparent purpose. However, it is only helpful to understand the process, not vital that we do.

But I do hope I have impressed upon you that the universe is, if nothing else, a very busy place. I also hope I've made the point that it is a far more complex and vast universe than we can begin to imagine, yet one in which not even the smallest detail goes unnoticed. Whether this leaves you with a sense of awe, shock, or even fear is a personal choice; as for me, it leaves me with a sense of comfort knowing that, despite the enormity of it all, everything works with absolute perfection. Nothing is wasted. There is no end to things (nor a beginning, for that matter), and, most significant of all, everything is meticulously and marvelously interwoven into a single, vibrant plan. It is a far more wondrous and expansive universe we live in, one that is beyond the abilities of even the best imagination to fathom, and the beauty of it is we never need to fear for tomorrow, for there is nothing that exists within its vast expanse that we haven't encountered untold times before. If that doesn't make the troubles of today pale in comparison to the magnificence of the eternal and never-ending journey of which we are all an integral part, I can't imagine what might do so.

chapter eight

The Roles of Time and Free Will in Reincarnation

Most people rarely consider time as a function of our existence. For most of us, time is a fleeting commodity that drives our lives, but not something we normally stop to think about. As such, it's easy to overlook its vital role with regard to how reincarnation makes spiritual progress possible, making it important that we take a moment to consider precisely how time works within this dual existence of the spiritual and physical realms.

So, what is the purpose of time? And, more important, how does it figure in to our quest for spiritual maturity?

Time is that which allows spirit to experience things on a practical level, and reincarnation is the process that spirit uses to put itself into time. In effect, time is the mechanism by which spirit lives, breathes, grows, and even "dies," all of which it cannot do—except on a purely conceptual basis—outside of time. Therefore, the spiritual realm needs the physical realm in order to exist as much as the physical world needs the spiritual realm to sustain it. They are mutually dependent upon one another, and time is the element that binds them together, despite the fact that only one of those worlds exists within the context of linear time.

Unfortunately, the tendency is to imagine that since the spiritual realm exists outside of time, there can be no concept of time within that realm. This, however, would be an erroneous assumption; while the spiritual realm does not operate with a clock on the wall, in being so closely entwined within the physical world of time and space, it is intimately involved with time even though it has no use for the stuff itself. While this may sound like a contradiction, it is not. Perhaps another analogy, which I personally find very useful to understanding paradoxes, is in order.

Imagine watching a movie and realizing that, though neither the character in the movie nor the audience knows what's going to happen next, from the perspective of the movie's director, what happens "next" has already happened months ago (or even longer if the movie is many decades old). Therefore, while from our perspective we don't know what's coming next, from a larger perspective "what's coming next" already came; we simply aren't aware of it because of our fixed perspective within linear time. We might imagine all kinds of potential scenarios ahead while watching the figures flickering on the screen in front of us, yet regardless of what we think *might* happen, what *does* happen is already preordained.

We can begin to get a better idea of how this timelessness works when we watch the same movie a second time. This time, instead of imagining what might happen next, we already know what is just around the corner, and it's the character (not the actor, but the character the actor's playing) that is *still* trapped in ignorance of his own future. In fact, each time you watch the movie you'll notice that the character *never* figures out why he shouldn't investigate the strange noise outside and repeatedly suffers the same grisly fate each time because of it. From our now-expanded perspective, however, we know what the character should or shouldn't do, but he remains eternally clueless, trapped as he is within his illusory celluloid world.

This is exactly the same situation we find ourselves in as long as we exist within the physical realm. We are a character acting within a movie who has no idea what's in store. The character in the movie, then, is the equivalent of the incarnated personality; the actor playing the role, however, who has already read the script and thus knows what's going to happen to his character, is the soul, who dutifully plays out the role even knowing what fate awaits and yet makes no effort to change it. The person watching the movie is the divine spirit or cosmic consciousness of the universe, who also manages to be the character, the actor, and the audience all at the same time.

However, even though the movie's director and actor are not operating within the timeline of the character in the movie, that doesn't mean they aren't aware that the movie itself has an external time meter, or that they can't work around it to effect other purposes. In other words, they are aware of time without being affected by it, which is, I believe, true of the spirit world as well. It may exist within time yet it does not experience it the way we do, nor is the soul bound to time in any way. Despite that, however, the soul takes time into account in its decision-making.

Even more interestingly, just as the director will make many movies over the course of her career, so too will the soul make many "movies" throughout the course of its "career." Additionally, just as the director can repeatedly view each movie she has made or even watch them all at once if she so chooses, the soul too is able to experience each incarnation repeatedly or all of them simultaneously if it chooses. They are in no particular order from the soul's perspective, though they may appear very precisely ordered from our viewpoint, which is a necessary illusion—all made possible through this mechanism known as time—if we are to perceive the benefits of multiple incarnations. In other words, we need to run the movies sequentially for them to make sense to us, which is why we generally assume that when we reincarnate we do so in a generally chronological order. This is all a part of the overall illusion, however; from the perspective of the spiritual realm, all our various incarnations are taking place simultaneously in the eternal "now."

This element of the rebirth process helps explain how the same soul can generate and insert two distinct personalities into the same time frame—in other words, how a person's past incarnation might still have been alive when he was born, leaving an overlap "between" incarnations. This is possible because the soul generates each incarnation into the circumstances that it considers optimal within which to have the experiences it desires, sometimes forcing it to generate the new incarnation prematurely. This overlap, however, does not impact the new personality.

This aspect of the rebirth process also brings up a curious question: if time is nonexistent from the context of spirit, we should not only be able to remember a past life but even "remember" a future incarnation as well, even though that future, at least from our perspective in linear time, has not occurred yet. In fact, if we work from the premise that time is not linear within the realm of the spirit, then the idea that we can look into our future should seem no more remarkable than should be our ability to look into the past. Yet it is the very illusion that events are occurring according to some sequential order that makes it possible to experience anything—past, present, or future—in the first place.

The Role of Personal Will

But this analogy brings up an important question: if the future is already preordained from the perspective of spirit, then what role does personal will play? In other words, if the director already knows what is going to happen to the character in the movie, then does the character have any will with regard to what happens, or is he eternally doomed to finish out the role, whatever it may be?

New Age writers consistently refer to the idea that the soul decides what is to happen in each incarnation and that therefore there are no such things as "accidents," since everything that is going to happen is effectively chosen beforehand by the soul. In other words, if a plane I'm flying on crashes and I'm killed, that was not an accident but part of the overall plan hammered together by my soul before I was even born.

Somehow I find this less comforting than some insist I should. Why would I choose such a morbid fate? For that matter, why would I choose to get cancer, get fired from a job I love, lose a beloved child to SIDS, or get a really bad haircut? It seems to me such an idea is nothing more than an effort to excuse every horrible thing that might potentially happen to me or someone I love as the "soul's plan," leading me to wonder if I might not be a more competent decision-maker than my own soul.

What we need to understand, however, is that just because the soul chooses to experience everything that happens to it, that doesn't mean it is making personal decisions about everything that might occur. What is really happening is that the soul permits the created personality to choose a particular path to embark upon, which it then chooses to accept, regardless of where that particular path it chooses to follow may lead. As such, if part of the chain of events we put into motion includes some misfortune or catastrophe, that is a natural element of that path, and so there is nothing "accidental" about it. The consequence was an inherent part of that choice, just as losing a leg to an exploding land mine is a natural consequence of walking onto a minefield, regardless of whether the decision to do so is made consciously or not.

What this has to do with time, then, is that in recognizing that while we are moving forward through linear time unaware of what awaits us in the future, the soul sees what's ahead but moves us toward it anyway—not because it's good for our spiritual development but because it is has, in effect, already happened. Whether we acquire any moral lesson or spiritual understanding as a result is beside the point; what awaits us is going to happen whether we learn from it or not.

Further, as a result of having free will within any incarnation, we have the option of changing the path we are moving down, thus simultaneously suspending the consequences and benefits inherent to one path while opening ourselves to an entirely new set of consequences and benefits inherent to a new path. By way of an illustration, imagine a man is walking along a path through a forest and comes to a fork in the road. If he chooses to take the road to the right, the path will lead him deeper into the forest; if left, the road will lead him eventually toward a small fishing village on the coast. Each path will afford him different possibilities—both positive and negative. One may lead to riches and fame, the other to destitution and hardship. Regardless, he must still make one of three choices: either to take the left fork to the sea, the right fork into the woods, or choose to do neither (which is also a decision). There is no "wrong" path in this context, only different paths. Which one he chooses will immediately close off one future—with all its possibilities, adventures, realizations, and experiences—while simultaneously opening up another; which one he chooses to take will completely shape one reality while extinguishing all the other theoretical realities.

From the perspective of eternity, however, the new path—with all its adventures and experiences—is already written, but so are the results had the other path been taken. Both and, potentially, countless more possible futures effectively exist at the same time. In other words, we have an infinite number of futures ahead of us depending on which choices we make—or fail to make—and each of those potential futures are, in effect, already realized. They already exist, just as the final outcome of a movie already exists. The only difference is that this movie has millions of different endings, and each one of them has already been shot and edited.

To bring this all together, then, when we step into a doomed airliner, the possibility that the aircraft may crash is but one of thousands of possible scenarios. That it does crash is the result of physical forces outside of our control (weather, structural failure, pilot error, and so on) and not a result of our conscious or even soul choice. It simply is one of the potential consequences inherent with all decisions, just as the plane's safe arrival after an uneventful flight is also one of the potential results of our decision to board the aircraft. In effect, then, we do not "choose" to die in an airliner crash, but we do choose to experience whatever eventuality plays itself out as a result of our decision to board the plane. Either result, however, be it a safe flight or a crash, has already happened from the context of eternity, and our soul on some level already knows it.

This may not be of much help to those who have lost friends or family to an accident, but once we come to the awareness that the soul is immortal and indestructible and has other adventures it needs to move on to, understanding how such a tragedy could have happened becomes, if not easier to accept, at least more understandable. It won't bring that loved one back, but knowing he or she has simply moved on to another context of existence as part of a greater agenda may soften the blow somewhat.

The Role of Randomness in the Process

Finally, another aspect of the life-growth process—and one that many people have trouble accepting—is the role that randomness plays in our spiritual development. To go back to our plane-crash scenario, the crash itself was not a preplanned event, either from the perspective of the soul or the personality that soul generated, but is a part of the equation known as randomness or—as some might call it—"luck" (which manifests itself as either bad or good, depending upon our perspective). I know this flies in the face of those who imagine everything that happens to be entirely a product of the soul's agenda or even a subconscious choice made by the personality on some deep level, but the fact is that there are events that occur with alarming frequency that are neither sought after nor desired, but which still play a vital role in each incarnation.

We will examine this idea of the role randomness may play in more detail in the next chapter, but for now it is sufficient to say that each life is an accumulation of both planned and unplanned events, the latter of which usually occur spontaneously in random order with little warning. These are things such as missed opportunities, good fortune, timely occurrences, and even pure dumb luck—each of which play more than a small role in each incarnation.

Of course, these events need not be only negative; in fact, there are just as many "happy" accidents as there are bad ones, so whether these random events that invade our lives are positive or negative is beside the point. What's important to understand is that randomness is figured in to each incarnation, just as is each conscious decision or soul desire. The problem comes in trying to determine which is which, as well as in determining what impact these chance experiences have on the path we have chosen.

For example, let's say that a man is having a dreadful time making a go of his business, with each business decision turning out to be worse than the previous one, until he appears to be on the verge of bankruptcy. Despondent and depressed, on his way home from work he impulsively purchases what turns out to be a winning lottery ticket with a massive payoff, thereby rescuing himself from potential bankruptcy. At the same time, another person is pursuing a promising career as a gifted musician, but it is all taken away from her when her car is hit by a drunk driver, injuring her so severely that she is no longer capable of playing her instrument, thereby robbing her of her future. What is going on here, and how do these events play into the process of spiritual maturation?

Both events were random to some degree (though purchasing the lottery ticket or the other driver choosing to drive inebriated were personal choices), but the results were life altering in both cases and, as a result, factored into the larger mosaic of each life. The only thing we have to be aware of is how they impact our lives in ways we may not even be aware of—as well as how they might impact the lives of others around us, also in both positive and negative ways.

I know this makes it sound as though the rebirth process appears to be entirely random—especially if both great luck and catastrophic misfortune are such an important part of it—but, in reality, randomness is actually one of the most important mechanisms of spiritual growth, for how we deal with the unexpected is the best barometer of where we are spiritually. For example, if the man who wins the lottery uses that money only to selfish ends, that will serve to highlight those areas of darkness in his soul that need to be addressed in the next incarnation. The injured musician, on the other hand, may find a new calling as a therapist to those who have been similarly handicapped, thereby demonstrating that her soul is further along than might have been apparent before the accident. In other words, we need randomness, for the lessons it provides us.

Conclusions

This should be enough to impress upon you that the process of spiritual growth is far from simple; in fact, it is a complex and even sophisticated dance that factors in many elements to make it work. Time, free will, and randomness are all part of that process and are what make it possible to bring about the maximum number of experiences each soul and—by extension—God can have via the mechanism of reincarnation. God is about the job of experiencing Himself in all His splendor and glory, as well as all His darkness and fear, none of which can be realized without all three elements—time, free will, and randomness—being factored into the mix. Take any part of that away, and the whole suffers as a result. That may not make life easier to understand or any easier to live, but it does help us appreciate why our lives are the way they are: we are all a part of God experiencing Himself in a myriad of ways we can only begin to imagine.

chapter nine

The Role of Evil in Reincarnation

We like to imagine the spirit realm as a place of light and love, which of course it is. Unfortunately, this makes it difficult to imagine how those attitudes or behaviors we perceive to be "evil" can coexist. After all, if God is love and God is all there is, then how can evil exist in any context?

Yet we know that evil exists, despite the best attempts by some to define it out of existence. Yes, it is a byproduct of fear and the sense of separation, but that makes it no less real nor does that mitigate the consequences we all experience as a result of it. To suggest evil isn't real is merely to play games with what is, in the end, a very important force within the process of reincarnation. Before examining this issue further, however, it might first be helpful to better define what evil is.

Evil is a word that everyone imagines they understand, yet when pressed for a firm definition it quickly becomes obvious that it has as many different meanings and applications as does the word *love*— another word that is so overused that it has lost nearly all of its true meaning. Generally, evil is thought to be an act—or, sometimes, an attitude—that is at variance with a society's generally agreed-upon set of moral imperatives. In effect, it is the position that there are certain behaviors, actions, or thoughts that the larger population in general considers to be so unacceptable and inappropriate as to be considered "evil."

This, however, is where things start to get tricky, for quite often what behaviors, actions, or thoughts the larger population considers to be evil vary from culture to culture and even from one era to another. For example, sexual promiscuity has traditionally been perceived to be an evil in most cultures, but what makes it so? The promiscuous person is engaging in an action—sexual intercourse—that is commonly done by the majority of adult human beings. If occurring within the traditional context of monogamous marriage, it is considered a natural and even a healthy form of human expression. Yet this same activity, when performed outside the social institutions of marriage and monogamy, makes the act evil. The act itself is technically no different whether performed within the context of marriage or in the context of a one-night stand, yet when done outside the properly designated social conventions makes it considered a sin by many and a great evil by some, thereby demonstrating that, in most cases, it is the culture that determines which things are to be considered good and which things are to be considered evil.

To further reinforce this point, suppose one lived in a society in which sexual expression of all kinds was given free rein. In fact, imagine that in this "culture of love" it was considered inappropriate— even sinful—to withhold the free expression of one's sexual nature. In this case, such a society would decide that evil resided in people's *refusal* to indulge their passionate nature as that nature demands. In fact, one could become a social pariah for insisting upon monogamy, and celibacy would be looked upon much the same way we tend to look upon promiscuity. In this case, everything we understand about the word *evil* would be turned on its head, and our sacrosanct definitions of good and bad would go out the window.

Additionally, the definition of sin or evil varies from individual to individual as well. Someone raised in a rigid, legalistic home might consider nudity in any context to be evil, while those raised in a more liberal environment might not be particularly offended by even the most graphic pornography. In fact, entire cultures alter their opinions of what constitutes evil, often with remarkable speed, simply as an element of their growth. For example, when I was a boy, cohabitation and premarital sex were considered great sins, while ethnic jokes and racism were widely practiced and at least tacitly accepted. Today unmarried couples who live together—both straight and gay—are increasingly accepted, while racially stereotyped humor and both overt and subtle racism are considered the great sins of our day. Of course, some actions remain unacceptable and are considered as evil today as they have been in the past, but for the most part society changes to fit the new moral dynamics of its age, both responding to the new mores and serving to reshape them at the same time. Definitions of morality, then, are constantly shifting and have been throughout history, with one generation considering another generation either irredeemably wicked and degenerate or hopelessly naïve, quaint, and old-fashioned.

Even if we accept, however, that tastes and morals shift from era to era and culture to culture, what about actions we normally consider universally evil, such as murder, lying, stealing, and rape? Doesn't this demonstrate that an objective standard exists?

Again, it's all a matter of context. Most people would agree that murder is always wrong, and yet in the context of abortion, capital punishment, self-defense, and armed conflict, murder is usually considered acceptable (though it usually is not labeled as murder; that is the value of euphemisms). It can be imagined that almost every act we define as "evil," then, might be considered acceptable—even "good"—by someone else, given the proper context. The point is that the carefully articulated standards of "right" and "wrong" we have spent so many centuries crafting for ourselves are largely illusory and subjective, making any definition of "evil" suspect at best and most likely impossible.

But what of the Nazis and the Holocaust, or Stalin's brutal gulags, or the genocides in Cambodia and Rwanda? Clearly these are great evils that can't be dismissed as mere cultural anomalies.

Again, it must be remembered we are looking at these events from a specific cultural perspective. The Nazis did not consider the so-called Final Solution to be evil (although we know a few of them had some misgivings about it), but considered it a means of improving the quality of life for the "Aryan" race by exterminating the Jews and other "subhumans" who they believed threatened the "purity" of the race. Stalin was bringing—from his perspective—stability and the fruits of communism to the masses, with the wholesale extermination of "traitors" and other undesirables being the necessary price to be paid for the socialist utopia to be eventually realized. Perhaps much the same mindset was even in play in Cambodia and Rwanda, as thousands were slaughtered for the "purification" of the state or the "safety" of the tribe.

The point is that whose perspective is right is always determined by the victors. Had the Germans won the Second World War and gone on to create a powerful and prosperous Third Reich as Hitler and his henchmen dreamed, the Holocaust would have been portrayed as a necessary—albeit unpleasant—step in achieving that goal. Further, had America lost the war, how would history have looked upon the dropping of atomic bombs on Hiroshima and Nagasaki—events that, like the Holocaust, also ended in the extermination of multitudes of innocent civilians? Even though these bombs were dropped in an effort to shorten the war—and therefore save countless lives in the process—would such a justification be accepted from the perspective of the victorious Axis powers? It is often only within the context of history that the final determination of whose action was "evil" and whose was noble is made, thereby skewing the entire definition of what constitutes good and evil.

So what does this do for our definition of evil? Are we to assume that since even the most heinous acts can be construed as right when seen through the "proper" perspective that there is no such thing? Not at all, for while our definitions are not necessarily universal or absolute, they are valuable in that they define us as a culture and as individuals. They make a statement about where we are collectively and personally on our spiritual path, and therefore are a necessary part of the process of growth. The Hitlers and Stalins of the world serve a function in that process, for they hold mirrors up to us and make us look hard at the reflections they cast. Hitler did not create anti-Semitism; it had been ingrained in European culture for many centuries. But the Nazis did show us what such an attitude, when given free rein and codified into a nation's laws, would look like in practice. The evil we do as a community and as individuals, then, while far from condemning us, merely reflects what we are on the inside. The ugliness does not reside in the mirror but in the visage of the person whose reflection it is.

Hitler and those like him gave humanity the opportunity to pause and carefully reflect upon our own attitudes, values, and beliefs. To our credit, we didn't like what it showed us about ourselves and we changed, yet would we have had the incentive to do so without the mass graves and cremated remains of millions of innocents? Hitler and the Nazis demonstrated like nothing else could what cruelty could be perpetrated upon humanity in the name of "progress" if we did not change our attitudes about anti-Semitism, racial superiority, or militant nationalism. It was a hard lesson that perhaps nothing short of a Holocaust could have taught us so quickly. Hitler and those "dark" souls like him showed us—albeit unintentionally—what a cancer racism can be if left untreated.

As such, it could be argued that without evil, spiritual growth would not be possible or even definable. If we have no racism to combat or despot to overthrow or, to use the most extreme example, an Auschwitz to get angry about, we have no context within which to understand goodness. There is no context by which good can be defined without evil; in effect, it is evil that defines good and vice versa. I suppose in the realm of pure spirit, goodness is all there is, yet I suspect it is our experiences on this plane of existence that makes it possible to appreciate goodness at all. In effect, it is Hell on Earth that makes Heaven so heavenly.

Unfortunately, this makes it seem that evil, then, is in a strange sort of way a "good" thing. In fact, we might even be tempted to argue that the more evil the better, for it will only enhance its opposite all the more. Evil behavior might even be encouraged, one could argue, to make Heaven all the more pleasurable. But such an attitude is looking at only half of the equation. Yes, evil does enhance the benefits and joys of goodness in much the same way that goodness is what makes evil so despicable. It is goodness that makes evil so despicable. It is selflessness that makes selfishness so unbecoming; it is the death of a "good" man that makes his murderer so reprehensible (notice how people rarely hold great animosity for the murderer of an "evil" man, even if done in cold blood).

More to the point, whether or not evil is beneficial to our spiritual progress is irrelevant, because those actions that we label as "evil" are an inevitable part of existence. Evil was not created by, nor did it come into the world through, Adam and Eve's disobedience in eating a forbidden fruit. It simply *is* and, presumably, always will be as long as sentient life takes on physical form somewhere in this universe. It is the price of existence and the cost of experiencing that existence. To wish it away or invent magic formulas designed to "wipe out" evil is futile, which is where religion ultimately fails. Evil cannot be destroyed any more than cold can be destroyed, leaving nothing but hot in its place, for the one cannot exist without the other. The point is not whether there is evil and whether we can or should do anything about it; the question is how does that which we define as evil define us, and how do we choose to respond to it? How you answer that will say more about yourself than anything else could.

Yet we still haven't defined what evil is from the perspective of spirituality, beyond suggesting that evil is what we decide it is. This, however, is an oversimplification. There are certain characteristics of evil that are unmistakable and generally definable, and are understood only as we define what spirituality is trying to teach us. Therefore, perhaps the best way to define evil is to look at every action, every thought, and every deed from the context of what spirituality or, more precisely, love is trying to do. In essence, all actions, thoughts, and deeds should be examined from the perspective of whether they encourage, enhance, and help us or others grow spiritually, or whether they impede or work against that goal. In other words, if I do such and such to you know who, will it help me achieve greater spiritual understanding and enlightenment, or will it arrest it? Notice, it's not a question of whether it will personally benefit me, or if it will be good for America, or whether it would make things easier for my family, but rather the question is: will it personally help or hinder me in my spiritual walk?

It is not about individual or collective gain, but spiritual gain, and spiritual gain may not be—and, indeed, often is not—personally or collectively beneficial. It may mean sacrifice. It may mean doing without or not being proven right or letting someone else have their way. It may be difficult—even nearly impossible. Yet when every decision, thought, and action is viewed through such a lens, the issue of good versus bad is less prone toward bias and subjectivity, at least if one is serious about evolving spiritually. If my decision is based upon what is best for my spiritual evolution, decisions of right and wrong become obvious. Which course we are to pursue comes from within. It is our heart that tells us—if we do not suppress or ignore it—which is the proper course of action in any given situation.

As far as I can see how it functions in the context of reincarnation, it seems to work something like this: we have already established that humans are nothing more—or less, for that matter—than the outward expression of an underlying soul. In essence, we are two-part beings: one part, the personality; and the other part, the soul or "higher self." Our personality—or ego, if you prefer—is what determines our conscious desires and constantly sets about pursuing them (often to our own detriment). Our soul, however, is determined to get for us what we require for spiritual growth rather than what we desire consciously. In other words, it is what tells us on a "gut instinct" level what we *need*, not necessarily what we *want*.

The soul, then, is interested only in spiritual growth in the same way that all living things are determined to grow. That's not to say it ignores the needs of the physical body, but spiritual growth comes when we give our highest, purest, and most giving instincts free rein, even when it means denying ourselves some earthly pleasure or possession. It is the price of evolution, but in the end it is well worth it, for there is a payoff: when we routinely endeavor to follow our highest instincts, eventually our physical, conscious nature learns to conform to the goals of the subconscious, spiritual nature—and a type of perfect emotional and spiritual unity follows.

Think of the personality as the child part of ourselves and the soul as the parent part. The child part wants all kinds of things it really doesn't need, often attaching great importance to genuinely trivial objects and pursuits. It hates to take no for an answer and pouts if it doesn't get its way. It throws temper tantrums and refuses to take responsibility for its emotional laziness. It believes the world owes it a living and imagines itself a good little boy or girl, loved by all.

All the while this is going on, however, the soul, like a patient and loving parent, is standing by, watching the child, giving it advice and gently leading it away from danger. It works behind the scenes, so to speak, quietly leading the child through the dangers and temptations of life, trying to protect it from its own stubbornness, ignorance, and foolishness. Most of what it does goes unrecognized by the child, who actually considers the parent a hindrance to its fun. Additionally, the parent is limited in what it can do. It must fight between its desire to protect and its desire to let the child learn from its mistakes. Sometimes the child wins out and the parent can only watch helplessly as it rebels toward its own destruction, but in most cases—especially if there is a desire for spiritual growth evident in the child—the little one will eventually grow into a mature and responsible adult.

Then, at last, just as a rebellious teenager sometimes returns to the wisdom and counsel of his or her parents later in life, the two halves form a close bond of mutual love and respect, the child now acting as a voluntary conduit for the wisdom of the parent. In effect, in highly advanced spiritual beings, the two halves merge to form a single whole, resulting in a perfect peace and contentment that is the essence of the Divine. That is enlightenment. That is nirvana.

Conclusions

I firmly believe most mental illness and dissatisfaction with life stems from the failure of our physical and spiritual natures to mesh, which is why we often seem to be at war with ourselves, both individually and collectively. This is not a battle between good and evil—though it frequently appears that way—but a battle between two wills: one toward fulfilling the desires of the flesh for physical pleasure, comfort, and security, and the other toward fulfilling the higher obligation toward spiritual development.

New Age beliefs teach a spiritual realm of light and love and that is probably the truest reality of what awaits the soul when it leaves the physical realm; evil, then, is simply a temporary and lesser energy that exists within the periphery of our senses, designed purely to showcase the magnificence of love, especially when contrasted with the dullness of evil. In the end, all souls—even the darkest among them—will be drawn back into the light, for that is all that finally exists within the realm of the absolute. The victory of light over darkness is already a reality, as it has been since the beginning; it is just that there are those few lost souls who need to find that out the hard way and thus choose to walk a much more difficult path than the rest of us. It is all a part of the process. It is all a part of existence.

chapter ten

The Karmic Dance

Perhaps no word in our culture has been bandied around with more abandon than has the ancient term *karma*. This has had the unfortunate consequence of rendering the word meaningless in many respects, ensuring that it serves as a type of catchall term for "payback" or "retribution." In fact, *karma* means much more than that, as we will see in this chapter.

Technically, karma is a Sanskrit word that simply means "action," and it is similar in many respects to the Western concept of cause and effect. Within Eastern thought is the belief that the things we do or experience in a previous life impact our present life in ways both subtle and severe, both in terms of our "station" in life and, in some cases, physically as well. For example, a brutal slave owner in a past life might find himself reincarnated as a slave; or a despot who enjoyed putting out the eyes of his enemies in a past incarnation may be born blind in a later incarnation to atone for his previous barbarity.

Since the human expectation that justice be served is universal, karma is not a difficult concept to accept even among those who have no belief in reincarnation per se. It does, after all, speak to the very basic human desire to see wrongs righted, either through temporal mechanisms of justice (i.e., incarceration, execution, restitution, etc.) or, if that fails, within the context of eternity (purgatory, Hell, rebirth into a negative incarnation, and so on). In fact, it is such a primordial instinct within the human species that it is difficult to imagine how any religion that does not address the issue of justice could be sustainable.

However, precisely how karma works is not understood by everyone in the same way. Like most belief systems, there are various schools of thought on the concept, many of which are either vastly misunderstood or largely unknown in the West. For the sake of clarity, we will examine the three chief justifications behind karma as generally taught, in an effort to understand the subtle but significant differences that exist between them.

Karma as Retribution

The most prevalent view of karma within both Hinduism and Buddhism is that it is primarily a mechanism designed to punish a person for past wickedness. It works from the premise that there is a "scale of justice" in place that demands sin debts be repaid, if not in one lifetime, then in another. In some cases, this retribution can be fairly mild—say a wealthy person being born into a poor family or an abusive husband being reincarnated as a woman—while in others it can be most severe (as in the above example of the evil despot reborn as a blind man). This assumption of retribution is why, within some cultures that embrace reincarnation, serious birth defects are often considered evidence of a wicked past life, while those born into great poverty and squalor are thought to be paying for an earlier life of selfish opulence and greed.

However, the question that needs to be immediately addressed before moving on is why we assume evil needs to be "paid for" at all. Further, is it even *possible* for evil to be paid for, either through the mechanism of retributive karma or through the traditional Western mechanisms of purgatory or Hell?

It seems an affront to some people to suggest that the wicked might not be punished in some way, as if retribution were the only thing that would set everything right. Unfortunately, it's a very human attitude that goes back to the dawn of time, when we sought retribution against the other tribe for their perceived wickedness while interpreting our own brutality as righteous indignation or, at very least, prudent self-defense. It's also the reason that punitive karma attracts us: not only does it justify ourselves to ourselves, but it helps maintain the illusion that justice can be served.

But what is meant by justice being "served"? Clearly, no wrong has ever been righted through punishing the perpetrator. To do that, the very act of retribution itself would have to have the effect of undoing the consequences of the evil act that was committed but, of course, we know it does not. If a person takes the life of another—either intentionally or accidentally—no amount of jail time (or even the death penalty itself) will undo that death. The victim's children, spouse, parents, friends, and family will still be without that individual, regardless of the severity (or, for that matter, lightness) of punishment the accused receives. Even if the criminal is executed, it makes no more difference to the ultimate outcome than if he were to get away with the crime scot-free.

While obviously a sense of justice does matter within the context of our present society and we should always strive to see that the human and civil rights of all people are secure, nothing we ultimately do in any single lifetime impacts eternity. The crimes we commit alongside the good deeds we do are reflections of our level of spiritual maturity; while they may have inadvertent repercussions within future lifetimes, in the context of the spirit realm they mean nothing. Therefore, punishment is not, in and of itself, a useful tool for spiritual growth.

A person may learn from being punished for a crime, it is true, but that lesson has to come from within the human heart; it cannot be impressed upon a person from the outside. That's why two men may be imprisoned for the same crime and one will truly repent and strive to change his ways while the other will simply regret having been caught. The key to spiritual growth is not in suffering a punishment but in recognizing what sort of person one is, and that can only come from within. Therefore, to punish a man for the crimes of his previous incarnation neither undoes anything he may have done nor does it teach either man anything new that might advance his spiritual development.

This may sound as if I'm suggesting we let people get away with their crimes, but I'm suggesting nothing of the kind. I'm simply recognizing the cold, hard fact that since everything we do is done within the context of linear time, there is no way to pay for anything that is done. We may apologize to our victims or even attempt to make restitution, but we cannot undo what has been done. It simply is not an option that linear time permits. Therefore, to punish someone in a future incarnation for crimes committed in a previous one is not only counterproductive but an immense waste of time that has no capacity to achieve anything useful. What has happened has simply happened. Karma cannot change that. It is not designed to.

Of course, it could be argued that the purpose of retribution is not to undo the past but to teach the soul not to keep doing the same brutal things over and over again through each successive incarnation. While this has some merit, it too fails to address the issue of just how the soul might change its nature by being punished. Punishment can modify behavior to some degree, but rarely does it change the underlying personality. The fact that recidivism rates for released felons within our prison system remain consistently high demonstrates that fact; punishment itself simply isn't capable of altering the human heart, so why do we imagine it might alter the human soul?

Further, punitive karma fails to take into account the negative circumstances that may surround a particular incarnation that was responsible for the direction the soul has taken through the course of a particular lifetime. Frequently, brutal and violent lives are the result of growing up in abject poverty or in a particularly militant or vicious culture in which aggressive tendencies are taught and encouraged. There are numerous external factors unique to any particular incarnation that often have less to do with the spiritual state of the soul than with the circumstances of one's birth. Does it make sense, then, to punish the future personality for the difficult circumstances of a past one?

Karma as Teacher

Another—and decidedly more popular—perspective on karma is that it is not primarily a means of exacting retribution but instead is better understood as a tool for teaching the underlying soul valuable lessons designed to enhance its spiritual development. While punitive karma is theoretically supposed to achieve the same thing, instructive karma really does attempt to shape the soul through finding useful circumstances it might use to experience a wider range of perspectives than would otherwise be possible within the course of a single lifetime. In other words, if the point of reincarnating is to apply the lessons from the previous incarnation to this present life in an effort to realize as rapid a spiritual growth as possible, then karma would seem to be the ideal mechanism to carry this out.

To see how this might be realized practically, imagine that the soul of a Nazi killed in the Second World War is forced to reincarnate as a Jew. In this way, it is supposed, the soul will experience life from a perspective it had not encountered before and so purge the poison of anti-Semitism from its blood, thus refining itself spiritually and growing toward ever-higher levels of understanding and awareness. Moreover, this need not be an unpleasant experience, for the lesson is realized whether the new incarnation's life is an easy or difficult one; in either case it is the experience of living life as a Jew that is beneficial to spiritual growth and not the specific circumstances of that life.

Additionally—the theory goes on to suggest—some souls may be born into decidedly unpleasant circumstances, but this is not done in an effort to punish the current personality for some previous evil, but precisely to learn lessons only those born into poverty or suffering from deformity, weakness, oppression, or sickness can appreciate. In other words, the soul may be induced to reincarnate into especially difficult circumstances because doing so will give it a fresh perspective that will prove vital in furthering its spiritual progress.

While this concept of karma is far more positive than punitive karma, it unfortunately suffers from many of the same problems, the most significant being the fact that just as in the case of punitive karma, instructive karma is equally lost upon the new personality. For example, just as a man may have no recollection of having been a vicious criminal in his past life, so too the Jew who was a Nazi in his previous incarnation also retains no memory of that anti-Semitic past, and without these memories there is nothing to be learned. In this scenario, one cannot appreciate what it is to be a Jew if one cannot also recall having been anti-Semitic, and so the former Nazi can learn nothing from his new incarnation. As far as both personalities are concerned, the other does not exist, at least within their frame of reference. While the Jew may retain some characteristics of his Nazi past, unless he has the requisite memories to go with it there is nothing to compare the new experiences to. The entire process remains pointless, at least within the context of linear time, if there are no residual memories to give the experience meaning.

Some counter this by claiming that it is the soul that is supposedly learning these lessons, not the personality, which is a valid point. However, even if it is the soul that is benefiting from the change of venue, it is still the present personality that is living out the soul's karmic direction and thus experiencing the consequences (or, for that matter, the benefits) of that venue, which brings up the issue of fairness. If one were to reincarnate in some positive venue, that's fine, but what if one returns as a muscular-dystrophy patient? Even supposing the soul is learning all kinds of valuable lessons from the experience, the personality it has manifested is still suffering—sometimes horribly. Suffering for the sake of the soul's spiritual enrichment may sound ennobling, but it is suffering nonetheless, and as such can have no place in the world of a loving divinity. To separate the soul from the personality is to concentrate on the rights of the one—the soul—at the expense of the personality, which renders the personality of no intrinsic value.

That souls may enter into difficult incarnations, then, may be a reality, but it is only an assumption that such incarnations are a result of some rigid karmic law that cannot be broken. The effects may be similar, but it seems far more likely such results are driven by choice rather than determined by karmic law, making karma as a tool for spiritual growth a result of faulty interpretations of external circumstances. In other words, while it may appear the soul has entered into a difficult incarnation in an effort to learn a lesson it needs to learn, the reality might be something quite different. It is merely our limited understanding of how the process works that makes us interpret things the way we do.

Karma as a Balance of Negative and Positive Energies

A third idea about how karma works maintains that, unlike the other concepts that see each incarnation as either an inevitable consequence of a prior life or the result of a carefully crafted plan, karma's role is that of an entirely indifferent and even morally neutral force that is not interested in either punishment or teaching, but merely in achieving spiritual balance. In other words, karma is simply a neutral mechanism of the soul by which negative energies are countered with positive energies in an effort to maintain a sort of spiritual equilibrium. It is not "planning" things out, but simply righting a wobbling spirituality the way one might straighten a crooked picture on the wall.

The idea here is that the soul is inherently perfect, and so when negativity—which is considered an imperfect element—creeps into the picture, karma sees to it that everything is put right again. From this perspective, since the soul is seen as a great factory that is constantly producing new personalities, once negativity enters into one incarnation, the soul simply produces another, more positive personality to offset the negative effects of the earlier personality until complete spiritual harmony is restored. The effects are similar to the concept of learning from one's past mistakes by introducing a new personality to an incarnation that applies those errors, yet it is done blindly and naturally, without personal planning or judgment.

The problem with this concept, however, like the other concepts of karma, remains the same: it is still the unaware personality that essentially pays for the spiritual imbalance the soul is attempting to correct. Even if one personality's avarice and greed could be offset by a life of deprivation and want in the next incarnation in order to restore spiritual harmony to the larger soul, this still victimizes the personality born into that poverty and as such remains an injustice that demands an explanation. It also doesn't explain *why* the soul requires itself to be spiritually balanced or how a life of deprivation in one incarnation might actually "balance out" a life of selfish indulgence in another. If the soul's purpose is simply to appreciate what it is—pure divine love—by experiencing being that which it is not (say, selfishness, greed, and indifference), then why does it require balancing at all? Isn't the experience itself sufficient to tell it all it needs to know?

And, finally, there is the problem of balancing out a positive energy with a negative one. If we work from the premise that the soul is seeking to keep its energy in perfect balance, shouldn't an especially positive incarnation be countered by an especially negative one, if we are to take this idea of spiritual balance to its logical conclusion? After all, it doesn't make sense that if you can push a picture a little too far to the right that you can't also push it a little too far to the left.

Why Karma at All?

So, clearly, all three explanations that attempt to justify the rationale behind karma appear to be lacking on several fronts. They fail as an effective means of retribution by punishing the innocent for the crimes of the guilty; they fail as a mechanism for enlightenment by teaching the required lessons to an unaware student; and they fail as a mechanism for balancing the soul's spiritual energy by both achieving that balance at the expense of the innocent and failing to justify the need for such balance in the first place. As such, we are left with the question as to precisely what role karma, in fact, does play in reincarnation—if any. In fact, to take it one step further, what if there *is no such thing* as karma? What if it simply doesn't exist, despite all the teachings to the contrary?

Few reincarnationists stop to ask themselves this question, preferring instead to accept whatever position personally appeals to them. Yet it is an important question to ask, for it is only in challenging the traditional teachings on a subject that we come to either understand it more completely or destroy it as a potential impediment to further learning. Such, I fear, is what must be done with the entire notion of karma.

It is perfectly reasonable to assume that since the point of reincarnation is to "know ourselves," the experiences of each lifetime should shape us in ways both subtle and dramatic. Therefore, as we move through each incarnation it seems inevitable that the vast number of experiences we've undergone will have much to say about what form our next incarnation may take. This concept, in fact, is a part of karma's counterpart teaching known as *dharma*, which is the notion that our underlying soul constantly improves as it moves through each incarnation, much as clay takes on a greater degree of refinement the longer it remains on the potter's wheel. And just as the imperfections and blemishes are constantly worked out of the clay through the natural process of the constantly turning wheel, dharma mimics this effect by serving as a type of spiritual bank account in which only positive characteristics are deposited while negative traits are discarded.

The problem lies in imagining this refinement process being realized only through a succession of preplanned incarnations rather than through means of a purely natural and spontaneous process. In other words, while karma maintains that a soul works out its refinement through a series of carefully orchestrated spiritual choices or—at very least—through the effects of some impersonal tit-for-tat process of balance or retribution, the reality may be that such a process is entirely unnecessary for spiritual growth to take place. If both conscious past-life recall and regression therapy tell us anything, they demonstrate that the process of rebirth is apparently random, exhibiting neither a balance between prior-life and present-life actions nor any meticulous and precise preplanning. A modern businessman, for example, may recount—in turn—having been an eighteenth-century cobbler in England, a rug maker in fifteenth-century Baghdad, an Indian girl in the ninth century, and a sailor in third-century Greece—but none of these lives have any apparent connection between them. The English cobbler is not seen to be balancing out any negative actions of the Arab merchant, nor is the Indian girl paying for the crimes committed as a third-century sailor. Instead, each incarnation is a collection of very ordinary and unrelated lives that collectively argue against most modern ideas about karma.

Only rarely does one find a potential link between a present incarnation and a past life, and these are frequently tentative at best. A person who, for example, suffers from chronic health problems and then recounts under hypnosis that he was a brutal and violence-prone husband in a past life might be thought to be suffering a kind of "payback" for the harsh treatment meted out to an abused wife in that prior incarnation. However, this "link" is purely an assumption based upon the notion that what goes around, comes around, whereas in reality the health problems may be more a matter of bad genetics than bad karma. It's more commonly the case that there is no apparent link between this life and a past one at all, and certainly nothing that might demonstrate a quid pro quo between the actions of one incarnation and those of the next.

That doesn't mean certain patterns might not emerge over the course of several lifetimes, but such patterns do not suggest anything approaching karma. They are more likely the soul's effort to either more fully examine a specific venue by repeatedly incarnating into similar circumstances, or evidence of a soul that has gotten itself "stuck" within a particular venue that it seems to be either unable or unwilling to break. In either case, there is no evidence a soul is attempting to offset or pay off some incurred karmic debt by incarnating into similar, difficult lives; it's more likely its repeated manifestations into difficult (or, at least, similar) circumstances is a result of the random process of rebirth.

Additionally, there is no clear evidence that any single incarnation is necessarily planned out, but instead each is a spontaneous result of a process that operates quite independently of free will. That's not to say the soul lacks any preferences for its next incarnation—it merely suggests that the soul doesn't need to plan out each incarnation, or balance its spiritual energy, or pay for its past errors, in order to mature naturally. It will do so as a matter of course, quite apart from whether the next incarnation is carefully planned or utterly spontaneous. The process of spiritual maturation will go on regardless.

To appreciate this better, consider that over the course of a soul's "life span"[9]—so to speak—it will incarnate scores or even hundreds of times before it reaches full maturity. As such, it is inevitable that it will experience almost everything imaginable to the human race—as both male and female and from the perspective of many races, cultures, social stations, and environments—*naturally*, without having to plan anything at all. A soul is going to incarnate into positive circumstances and negative ones repeatedly, know difficult lives and fairly easy lives, and experience life from the perspective of a sinner as well as that of a saint many times before it is through, each of which will further shape its development.

If it's helpful, you can imagine reincarnation as a slow and steady but random process in which the benefits are seen over the long term rather than immediately. For example, over a series of ten incarnations a soul may find itself aborted, stillborn, or dying in infancy in three of them; existing in negative circumstances with little or no spiritual

---

9. Of course, a soul cannot die, so "life span" is an inadequate description. I simply mean here the time it takes for the young soul to grow to complete maturity before returning to its divine source.

growth in three others; and experiencing growth of a kind in the remaining four incarnations. Overall, the soul has matured in four of the ten incarnations—the four "positives" offsetting the three "negatives" and the three false starts. And since the positives are retained into the next incarnation while the negatives are purged, the soul still comes out ahead despite achieving a degree of spiritual growth only 40 percent of the time.

But what of the negative incarnations? Certainly it can be argued that reincarnating as a criminal or a murderer—regardless of whether it is preplanned or accidental—would be detrimental to spiritual growth. With enough such negative incarnations, isn't one potentially capable of moving further away from spiritual maturity and ever deeper into darkness? In effect, couldn't the entire process fail?

That we may occasionally manifest under circumstances that are less than ideal for spiritual development may appear on the surface to suggest such a thing; even those incarnations we might consider "failures" are, in fact, a part of the growth process. They are what show us where we are on our path and help us to appreciate the value in striving to move ahead. As such, there is no such thing as failure in the absolute sense of the word, for even failure is a necessary part of the process. In effect, we cannot ultimately fail, since failure is already figured in to the mix.

Consider it this way: when an inventor is working on a new invention he may initially encounter numerous setbacks, failed attempts, and dead ends. It is recorded that Thomas Edison tried literally hundreds of different materials as a filament for the light bulb before finally hitting upon magnesium. In the process, most of the materials he tried did nothing or immediately incinerated, while a few would burn brightly for a few seconds as electricity surged through them before burning out. Yet these were not failures in the strictest sense of the word, for Edison was working from a process of elimination. Each carefully recorded failure actually brought him one step closer to finding a substance that would work, permitting him to finally develop a practical light bulb and revolutionize the world.

It is the same for the soul that is striving for spiritual growth. It may frequently turn out to be a two-steps-forward, one-step-back process, but it is ultimately moving ahead toward its own perfection. That this progress may be achieved through a process of randomness makes it no more or less efficient than if it were carefully planned and, in fact, may make it an even more valuable process precisely *because* it is so random.

As such, we don't need karma to explain the mechanism of rebirth or even of spiritual evolution, for both are a byproduct of randomness. That's not to say a soul may not have some choice in its next incarnation—at least in general terms—or that these incarnations are not instructive and useful toward maturing spiritually, but that they need not be preplanned to be either. They simply are useful in the same way any new experience is an opportunity for growth and maturity—within reincarnation as well as within life in general. One need not carefully plan out every detail of a vacation to find it an educational or enjoyable experience; in fact, sometimes too much planning can be an impediment to experiencing anything truly interesting. There is something to be said for spontaneity, after all. Could this not be the case with reincarnation as well?

Conclusions

The belief that karma is a tool for spiritual development appears to be, at least when examined from the context of pure reason, a nonstarter. It simply is an unnecessary appendage where spiritual growth is concerned and, in some cases, may actually prove an impediment to appreciating the remarkable effectiveness and perfect function that lies at the heart of reincarnation.

While it seems undeniable that past lives may occasionally, and sometimes substantially, impact our present incarnation, for the most part the lessons they teach are far too subtle for the present psyche to appreciate. Reincarnation incurs spiritual maturity through a long, drawn-out process that is seen only in hindsight, its effectiveness in maturing the human soul the result of a cumulative process over eons of time and through countless incarnations. Human beings are, by nature, an impatient lot who want to appreciate the benefits of the process immediately. Reincarnation, however, is a timeless, ageless, and eternal process that feels no such urgency. If it takes a hundred incarnations to accomplish even a tiny bit of spiritual progress, the soul is as content as if it achieved the same results in just ten. The point is not to see who can finish first, but who can finish best—the prize in this case going not to the swiftest, but to the most determined, persistent, and patient.

chapter eleven

Old Souls and Soul Mates

Before leaving the topic of the soul and how it may function, it is first necessary to tie up some loose ends, and one of those is to answer the question why, if we are all just little "bits of God" masquerading about as human beings, we can't seem to get along with the other "bits of God" out there. If we are all a part of the larger cosmic consciousness we call God, then it seems that we should get along considerably better. The fact that we frequently don't, then, is something of a mystery.

The reason some souls seem peaceful, loving, and compassionate while others appear cynical, selfish, and hateful, however, is not all that difficult to understand if we approach the subject from the perspective of spirit. The answer to this riddle lies in understanding that the reason some personalities hate while others love lies not in their basic nature but in their spiritual "age," or maturity level.

This is sometimes a source of considerable confusion to some people. How could one soul be "older" than another? If all souls emanate from God and God is, by definition, eternal, how can there be such a thing as a "new" or an "old" soul, since all souls are technically the same "age"? It simply doesn't make sense.

The answer is that while our soul age is eternal, that doesn't mean that each soul has had the same number of experiences within physicality as others. If we work from the premise that all souls start out as blank slates, so to speak, and that each subsequent incarnation adds to its cumulative base of knowledge and understanding, then we must recognize there are likely souls further along in this process than others—those who have made more journeys into physicality and thus are more experienced or practiced in their spiritual understanding and awareness. There are souls we might consider to be more spiritually mature than others—that is, souls that have incorporated the lessons multiple incarnations have taught them and incorporated them into their present personality—making them, in effect, "old" souls. This, however, is as one would expect, because in order for divinity to experience all aspects of life, it is necessary for it to see through the eyes of both the wise and the frightened with equal clarity. Anything less would be to see only in one dimension and therefore miss the point of the exercise entirely.

Voyage to the Bottom of the Sea

To better illustrate this process, let's imagine the sky to be a metaphor for the spiritual realm and the ocean to be a metaphor for the physical world of linear time and space. Now, within the sky exists all manner of various gases that collectively make up what we call air. Further, this air exists everywhere and is not confined to one part of the sky; in fact, since it is air that makes up the atmosphere in its entirety, the air exists as a single unified entity without beginning or end. It has always existed and will always exist, for it is indestructible and eternal in all respects.

However, in order for the air to experience itself for what it is, it must separate from the sky for a time and be apart from what it naturally is, and it does this by choosing to enter the depths of the great ocean—that is, the world of physicality—where it will no longer be light and free and unified but will experience heaviness, limitation, and darkness. Driven by a massive pump through high-pressure hoses to an outlet on the sea floor thousands of feet below the surface, there the tiny pocket of air emerges in the cold blackness of a sunless, alien world confined within the thin walls of a bubble. Leaving the hose under great force (the birth experience), the "air" (or soul)—now encased within its own bubble—immediately begins making its way back to the surface, not by its own choice but because it is drawn to the surface, since it is lighter than the surrounding water and thus naturally buoyant. It also chooses to make the journey to the surface because it desires to return to the freedom and pure ecstasy of sky and sun from which it originated.

However, before it can reach its home in the sky, it must first pass through many thousands of feet of inky blackness, during which time it will experience its separateness from the sky above and, indeed, from the thousands of other bubbles traveling alongside it toward the surface. In this unfamiliar and uncomfortable state, it will feel itself to be utterly alone within its tiny bubble and so, for the first time, know fear and hopelessness.

It is not an entirely unpleasant experience, however, for eventually, as the bubble continues to rise toward the surface, it begins to notice the darkness melt away as sunlight is able to penetrate the depths. Further, as its surroundings brighten, the air trapped within the bubble begins to understand its true nature and soon realizes it no longer requires the limiting, encumbering bubble that has surrounded it all its life. Eventually it comes to look forward to shedding its restrictive, though not entirely unpleasant, prison and returning to its natural state. Perhaps as a result of this realization, the air within the bubble notices the water begin to shimmer with beautiful shafts of azure, green, and turquoise as the surface rapidly approaches, and for the first time the bubble begins to appreciate the breathtaking beauty of the ocean around it.

Finally, the bubble reaches the surface and, its shape no longer determined and maintained by the weight of the water pushing at it from all sides, bursts and releases the air inside it. At last free of the bubble, the air rejoins the rest of the atmosphere in joy and jubilance, excited to be home once again, its long journey from the depths of the ocean complete. Eventually it may choose to make the journey again, but for the time being it is at peace and enveloped in a world of love all its own.

Of course, this isn't a perfect analogy, for even within the atmosphere air is made up of individual atoms of various gases and these are separate from each other, but for our purposes I think it adequately illustrates my point: each "bubble"—each soul—starts its journey in darkness and fear but eventually finds its way to the light of the sun, growing in awareness and joy, through multiple incarnations, as it draws closer to the surface. The other point is that the "pump" is constantly pulling air into the long hose arching toward the ocean's bottom and thus releasing new "soul bubbles" all the time. Therefore, while the air inside each bubble may all be the same age, the age of each bubble is not; some are newer bubbles that have just begun their ascent while some are older bubbles that have been making their way toward the surface for a very long time. Also, since the size of a bubble determines its degree of buoyancy, some move upward much faster than others, reaching the surface sooner than many of the bubbles that were released before it do. Yet all will eventually reach the surface—even the smallest among them—and so complete the journey they set out on.

It is these older "bubbles" that we often refer to as "old" souls, and they are a natural and important part of the process, for they are the ones helping the "younger" souls reach the surface. They are the seasoned veterans of the spiritual realm who are not only willing but in fact eager to help others on their journey, just as there were those who were willing to assist them in their journey.

How do you identify an old soul? That's a good question, for they are not always easy to spot. At the risk of being presumptuous, however, I would postulate that old souls should possess certain common characteristics that set them apart from younger souls. For example, seasoned by dozens of lifetimes of toil and tribulation, they have learned tremendous patience, are peaceful and not easily perturbed or flustered, and most of all know how to love and laugh and live in joy. They are those people one sometimes encounters who have a perspective on life that is different from most other people—individuals who have a calmness, an inner peace, and a wisdom about them that seems well beyond their years. They are rarely fearful, worried, or angry, but instead have a built-in resiliency that seems almost otherworldly. They may not be well-educated or wealthy or even particularly religious; in fact, they are frequently simple, plain folk who live rather ordinary— even mundane—lives. Yet even in the midst of life's trials and disappointments, they possess an inner peace and steadfast calmness that emanates from them like a lighthouse beacon. They truly enjoy life as much as they enjoy people and seem capable of being entirely at peace whether they live in a mansion or a mud hut.

I have met people like that, and you probably have as well. They are the end result of many lifetimes of hard "spirit building" work. They are the ones we look to as reminders that the long journey through the darkness into the light may not be an easy one, but they teach us that no matter how frightening the journey may sometimes appear, it is one well worth taking.

In addition to helping younger souls mature, old souls serve a vital function on a macroscopic scale as well, serving as the impetus behind every great forward stride humanity has taken toward its collective enlightenment. For example, the abolition of slavery may not have been possible until enough old souls jointly decided that slavery was no longer an acceptable way to treat human beings and, through the sheer force of their will alone, were able to convince enough young souls to follow them and abolish the hated practice. As such, some of the greatest abolitionists in history may have been old souls (despite their shortcomings in other areas). Human rights activists, peacemakers, political dissidents, spiritual teachers, civil-rights leaders, physicians, and caretakers, along with many of those who strive to make a more peaceful, just, and compassionate world, are often old souls who are determined to make a difference and alter the face of society.

Many may give their lives in the process; others will sacrifice careers, family, wealth, and even peace specifically to drag society a little further along the road toward enlightenment, but that is how the process of reincarnation is supposed to work in altering entire worlds. Old souls do not look to escape the brutalities of this world but instead seek to change the world so that brutality disappears from its face. Though old souls often fail and are sometimes crushed beneath the heel of a dictator's boot, their capacity to shape the direction of society is considerable, and they are relentless in their task. Unfortunately, their success is frequently seen only in hindsight many centuries after the fact, but their effects are felt and will continue to be appreciated in the coming centuries as humanity strives to pull itself out of darkness and into the light of its own divinity. That is only one of the positive byproducts of reincarnation, and one of its most important.

Defining and Understanding Soul Mates

Even among people who do not believe in reincarnation, the idea that there exists within the universe that one person designed specifically for them is more than just grist for romance novels; the idea is a common notion within our culture, despite finding its basis within Eastern reincarnationist beliefs. This, of course, is the concept of "soul mates" that has been such a popular theme in contemporary Western culture over the last several decades.

The idea works from the premise that if we accept reincarnation as a fact, it is therefore likely we have closely interacted with hundreds or even thousands of people over the scores of incarnations we've experienced, and so it should come as no surprise if we occasionally encounter one of these souls at some point in this present life. As such, when we form a particularly close friendship or love relationship, it is often romantically imagined that we do so because we knew this person in some past incarnation and our natural bond with them today is simply a continuation of that past relationship. Some even take this to the point of imagining that most, if not all, of their present relationships—including siblings, spouses, parents, close friends and, on occasion, even business partners, colleagues, and employers—continue to move from incarnation to incarnation alongside of us, much like a flock of geese making the same trip south each winter.

In essence, some imagine we reincarnate in "packs" through countless incarnations, and it is these fellow sojourners to whom we are most naturally attracted. Of course, not every "soul mate" may appear in every one of our incarnations, even as we may not be a part of each of theirs. As a rule, however, most of them are generally a part of each incarnation, though they may take on vastly different roles. For example, someone who may have been your son in one incarnation becomes a close colleague in this one, while your current spouse or partner may have been your parent in a previous incarnation.

The reason many people have no trouble accepting this idea is because we have all shared the common experience of meeting someone for the first time and being immediately and inexplicably drawn to them for no apparent reason. This isn't merely a question of sexual attraction (love at first sight) but something deeper: an almost instant rapport and easy familiarity that seems firmly established though we have only known the person briefly. The friendship and attraction, in other words, is not only instantaneous but feels instinctively natural, as if you have been reintroduced to an old friend you haven't seen for many years and are simply picking up where you left off.

That we are likely to encounter familiar souls from previous incarnations seems reasonable, and that souls might travel in packs also is not without some logic. The problem is that most people understand the concept from a purely positive perspective; yet if there is such a thing as soul mates (or, as I prefer, familiar souls) this should also work in a negative context as well. For example, we have all suffered through difficult relationships at some point in our life, from an adulterous spouse to a traitorous co-worker to an unreasonable and demanding boss. Therefore, it is reasonable to imagine we may also encounter some of these same souls again just as easily as we may encounter those with whom we had a positive relationship in a past life and, further, that they may evoke the same kinds of negative feelings in this incarnation as they elicited in the last one. Just as most of us have encountered people we had an immediate affinity for, most of us have likewise met people we immediately took an inexplicable disliking to, for no obvious reason.

This instant dislike is more than a result of a person's arrogance or condescending attitude, but is enmity for no apparent reason. Further, it is often felt far more strongly and intensely—sometimes even to the point of hatred—than one would reasonably expect to feel toward a person who is simply unpleasant, uninteresting, or otherwise unlikable. Is it any less likely, then, that such people may have been protagonists from previous incarnations? After all, if we do travel together through each incarnation, we must assume that at least a *few* of our fellow "incarnates" are people we've had negative dealings with in previous incarnations.

Ironically, if true, these "dark souls" (for want of a better term) may be, in some ways, more important partners in our spiritual quest than those we count as "light souls," for they possess the capacity to refine us far more sharply and quickly than those positive souls from the past we meet again. For example, we can only learn patience with someone who tries our patience, so those negative souls we've known from past lives may be more useful than we might imagine. Moreover, we may be useful to them in their spiritual development as well. In fact, we might be someone else's nemesis from a previous incarnation without even being aware of it. Consider this the next time you have a boss who is more than you can handle or a mousy, conniving co-worker you can barely stand working next to; you both may be helping each other toward spiritual maturity without even realizing it!

While the concept of soul mates is an interesting idea and prob-ably—at least to some degree—a valid one, it is easy to overdo it. With the huge number of people we encounter over the course of a single lifetime, we do not require souls from the past to make our experience in this lifetime any more challenging or fulfilling. Though it is possible and, for that matter, even likely that some souls form bonds that transcend each incarnation—just as there are lifetime friendships capable of withstanding the test of time—we should not assume everyone with whom we have some significant dealings is a past-life acquaintance.

Spiritual growth is about encountering a wide range of people in order to realize the fullest range of experiences possible; while a repeat relationship from a previous incarnation might prove helpful and even mutually beneficial, it is in new relationships that we move beyond our past to grow in new and unexpected ways. Insisting that we pursue relationships only with the familiar souls of our past could be even something of an impediment if taken to extremes, especially if it results in our overlooking the opportunity to forge new bonds with those "first-timers" we might encounter in this incarnation. Spir-itual growth results from interacting with a mixture of past-lifetime acquaintances we have known and those we meet in the present who have new lessons to teach us; it is important to maintain a balance between both groups.

chapter twelve

Between Incarnations

If one accepts reincarnation as a postmortem reality, it seems there can be no greater question than what happens to us between each incarnation. Do we exist in some kind of limbo state to await our next excursion into the physical world, or do we—as some suggest—experience a kind of "life review" in which our time on Earth is carefully and exhaustively examined? And, finally, what of Heaven? Is there room for such a place within the mechanism of reincarnation, or is the idea of an "eternal reward" nothing more than a mythology invented by Western religion?

There are a number of ideas about what happens to our soul between incarnations, each of which has its proponents and detractors. We will examine each in turn to determine their plausibility, but in the end it should be understood that all such musings must remain purely speculative. Unlike past-life memories with their occasionally verifiable details to ponder, we have very little to go on when it comes to this particular question. Since the intermediate state between incarnations is seldom examined in any great detail by therapists,[10] the question of precisely what happens during this period remains largely unexplored (and, perhaps, unknowable). As such, much of what we discuss in this chapter, like much of this book, must remain purely conjectural—though not outside the realm of logic.

The Limbo State

The first and perhaps most frequent assumption many make is that nothing happens between incarnations—we simply die and immediately look for another fetus to inhabit. Many Eastern faiths adhere to this notion, as do some New Age purveyors, while research into conscious past-life memories in children by noted reincarnationist investigator Dr. Ian Stevenson suggests this possibility as well, for he has found almost no memories of any intermediate state among his subjects. Instead, most who recall their previous death usually attest to having almost immediately—sometimes within months or even mere weeks of their death—found another fetus to inhabit.[11]

Yet there are a few cases in which some information about the intermediate state emerges, though such memories are often unclear and confusing. They do give the impression, however, that the personality is conscious and aware during this time, though how active it is tends to be is a matter of individual proclivity. Perhaps the best known of these is the celebrated (and subsequently pilloried) Bridey Murphy case, the alleged pre-incarnate personality of Virginia Tighe and the subject of the 1956 bestseller *The Search for Bridey Murphy*. She recounted being conscious after her death in 1864 and existing as a disembodied spirit, capable of seeing others in the physical world but

---

10. One noteworthy exception is Dr. Michael Newton, a professional hypnotherapist from California, who has written a number of books on the "in-between" state (see the bibliography of this book). He describes a sophisticated and fairly complex in-between state complete with guides, counselors, and carefully preplanned incarnations, some elements of which we will examine in more detail in this chapter.

11. However, Stevenson never hypnotized any of his subjects to determine if they might have some intermediate-state memories locked away in their subconscious.

being unable to interact with them. She also recounted speaking with the spirits of others she had known in life, though even then there appeared to be no real substance to their encounters. In essence, "Bridey Murphy"—though apparently conscious and perceptive—seemed to simply drift along with no real point or purpose in the aftermath of her death until finally landing within the body of the woman later known as Virginia Tighe in 1923, almost sixty years later.

So why are such intermediate-state memories so conspicuously absent or—at best—prosaic, during past-life regression sessions?

Beyond the possibility that nothing is recalled because nothing happens—the limbo-state theory—is the very real possibility that what happens during that period is a very personal and private affair of the soul to which the conscious personality is not always privy. In other words, what occurs may be happening on a higher "soul level" than that upon which the personality resides. Much as important corporate decisions made behind closed doors are not known to the average employee, so too might the experiences and decisions of a past life be examined and considered on a higher level—memories of which do not make it into the conscious mind of either the previous or present personalities. As such, during a past-life regression session the previous personality—now speaking through the present personality—really doesn't recall what occurred between the two lives, because the lessons learned and the decisions made were made on a "soul level" and not a "personality level." In essence, the personality doesn't remember what happened because it didn't happen to the personality; it happened to the soul. The events of a past life might be easily recalled because they are a part of the personality; the lessons they taught the soul, however, are not retained by the personality but are known only to the "higher self"—the soul—and thus cannot be as readily accessed.

If this is the case, the personality might well not retain any between-life memories and might, in fact, seem to be (at least from its own limited perspective) merely drifting between incarnations, when in fact an entire process of life review and planning is going on elsewhere within the spiritual realm—a process that the personality is entirely unaware of. "Bridey Murphy" recalled a period immediately after her death during which she attempted to interact with the physical world and carried on only the most superficial contacts with a few others who had preceded her in death, but this period appears to have been short-lived. The next thing she recalls is being reborn in the body of an infant girl in 1923. But could something more have occurred during this interval as well, something of which even her own subconscious was unaware?

Heavenly Rest?

If we assume that the soul is conscious during these intermediate states—even if the experiences of this period may be inaccessible to us even under hypnosis—the question must be asked what possible environment might the conscious soul find itself in during this period? Is it a joyful environment, a contemplative one, or even a mundane one? And as I asked earlier, what of Heaven—or Hell for that matter?

One of the great hopes and comforts to most people is the idea that when they die their soul might wing its way to Heaven to be reunited with loved ones who passed on before them and so live throughout eternity in a state of bliss. In fact, one of the most common complaints about reincarnation I've encountered is that being reborn into the flesh—having to "come back"—effectively "robs" people of their eternal reward. I've know people who were prone to dismissing the entire concept of reincarnation entirely on that basis alone.

That the idea of Heaven is somehow inconsistent with reincarnation is, however, incorrect. Reincarnation does allow for such a state of existence, though there are some significant differences in how the concept is interpreted between Western religionists and reincarnationists. The basic differences are twofold: first, reincarnationists do not believe Heaven is a reward one acquires for living a "good" life—or Hell a punishment for an "evil" one—but that the soul returns to Heaven, which is normally described in New Age literature as a place of light and joy and peace, because that is all that exists within the spiritual realm. In other words, the soul goes to Heaven simply because there is *no place else to go*, making Heaven and the spiritual realm virtually synonymous terms.

The second significant difference between the Heaven of Western religion and that of the reincarnationist is that for the former, Heaven is eternal; once a person dies, his or her soul effectively remains in this blissful state forever, its brief sojourn on Earth nothing more than a distant and rapidly fading memory. For the reincarnationist, however, Heaven is only a temporary abode—a place of rest and reflection where the soul not only creates its own environment but recognizes that, like a wonderful vacation, it must end at some point and the soul must return to the "salt mines" of physicality.

While it's unknown how all this actually works, the idea that the soul is at rest while in the spiritual realm makes sense. This would seem especially true if the soul had just experienced an especially trying or traumatic incarnation and needed time to readjust and reflect upon what had just happened as well as acclimate itself to its new environment. Then, once refreshed, it may be ready for a return to the world of physicality to continue the process.

Additionally, the idea that this period is temporary is also misunderstood. From the soul's perspective, it may in fact appear to be transitory, but from the confines of the personality the soul had previously manifested—a personality that now exists completely outside of the venue of linear time—it may well *appear* eternal. In reality, time itself is illusory, making any reference to "temporary" and "permanent" meaningless, though these illusions are necessary for both the soul and the personality to perceive anything. As such, it remains entirely consistent to imagine that Heaven is a temporary abode of spiritual rest as well as an eternal state, depending upon one's perspective and whether the place is viewed from the context of a single personality or from the much larger context of the soul.

Before leaving the subject of Heaven entirely, it might be a good idea to mention something about Hell as well. While the idea of Hell as a place of eternal torment for wicked souls, as taught by Western religion, is clearly incompatible with a God of love and a spiritual realm of light and joy, the idea that a personality may experience anger, rage, and hatred during the intermediate state is also a distinct possibility. It is not unreasonable to imagine that people who die in darkness may hold on to their negative energy to such an extent that they find it impossible to experience the endless bliss of the spiritual realm and so remain locked in a kind of "dark limbo" state for a time, which may lead them to experience something very close to a hell. How long they remain there is up to them, but it may well be a considerable amount of "time" until they either find the means of working their way out of the darkness or are assisted by other souls to work their way out of the maze they have created for themselves.

Hauntings may be good examples of a personality that has refused to let go of its previous incarnation and so remains trapped between two worlds, where it will remain until it either tires of the torment it is putting itself through or is finally shown the way out. As such, while there is no Hell in the absolute world of spirit, we are each capable of manufacturing our own Hell and keeping ourselves imprisoned within it by our own obstinate refusal to let go of the past and turn to the light. Again, it is all a matter of personal choice—in the spiritual realm just as it is here in the physical.

The Life Review

While some reincarnationists doubt that a soul remains consciously active in the intermediate stage and others accept Heaven as the soul's intermediate estate, most manage to include somewhere within this period a time for reflection or review of the life just lived. To some, this may be a fairly simple process of careful self-evaluation while others claim that a far more complex process awaits the recently deceased soul. Edgar Cayce, whom we discussed earlier, maintained that a rather elaborate process of life review between incarnations takes place, during which the entire time just spent on Earth is reviewed and studied,[12] and suggestions are made by spiritual guides or counselors as to what the soul should attempt to achieve during its next incarnation. This idea is further reinforced by many of the intermediate-life studies carried out by Dr. Michael Newton and recorded in his popular books, including *Journey of Souls: Case Studies of Life Between Lives*.

This idea of an intermediate life review is popular among New Agers and many who believe in reincarnation in general, and it possesses a certain logic that makes it hard to ignore. After all, it makes sense that one would want to review past triumphs and mistakes if spiritual progress is the purpose of reincarnation, so it seems logical that some sort of appraisal be made. While it's possible that such self-appraisals do not occur simply because the events of a past life are no longer important to the growing soul—just as what happened to a person in second grade may no longer be relevant when that person is a forty-year-old adult—it seems more likely that the personality would retain some sort of conscious memory of its time on Earth, and, further, it is logical it would still maintain the ability to judge and weigh its own actions while on Earth in the light of its new spiritual environment.

So, if a life-review process does take place between lives as many profess, how might it work exactly? Certainly the idea of reliving one's more embarrassing or dishonest moments might be cause for some trepidation and even fear. This would especially be true if, as Newton and Cayce maintain, this review process is done under the auspices of spiritual guides or advisors. Of course, it needn't be a purely or even largely negative experience, for there is no reason to imagine that the more positive aspects of one's life might not also be examined alongside the negatives and progress pointed out where evident. In fact, in many cases the entire process might be an encouraging and even joyful experience though, obviously, that would depend upon the quality of one's previous incarnation.

---

12. Cayce maintained that this review was done at a central library-like facility known as the Hall of Akashic Records, where books containing the events of each life were kept and studied. This idea has worked its way into much New Age literature, though the concept did not originate with Cayce himself.

While all of this is purely speculative, I wonder if the pain or pleasure of such a process might not be entirely dependent upon the spiritual state of the soul being reviewed? In other words, a more advanced or mature soul might well perceive this process in an objective and balanced manner—seeing its past-life mistakes as opportunities for growth and a part of the sometimes painful process of maturation—while a less mature soul might perceive a life review from an emotional perspective, making the process of review an excruciatingly painful experience.

What's important to recognize in all this, however, is that while this life-review process may appear on the surface to be not unlike the concept of Judgment Day articulated in most religious literature, it is not designed to condemn or punish but to help us grow spiritually. It may feel unpleasant at points and even embarrassing to those personalities who are still "ego heavy," but in the end each life lesson is a chance to grow. As such, even a "negative review"—so to speak—would be handled with compassion and gentleness, especially in the realm of spirit. Aware of the trials and tribulations of each life, the environmental factors that shaped that life, and the general level of maturity of the soul involved, the "reviewers" (for lack of a better term) understand the reasons that an incarnation proved to be so problematic and would likely try to get the young soul to understand as well. There is not an effort to punish or humiliate the soul, but only to grade the progress each soul is making through each incarnation. There is no pass or fail in this test, only what happened and what might be learned from it.

Reincarnation is not interested in ridiculing, belittling, or otherwise humiliating us into changing, but simply in showing us where we are and how far we have yet to go. In its purest form, it is an optimistic and enlivening process, for it continually points us toward the direction our heart truly desires to go—in the direction of joy, peace, and love. It may seem a stern and even cruel master at times, but in the end we will emerge from the process thankful for the patience and gentleness it has shown. It is, after all, simply the process of the soul redefining itself and, in the course of doing so, moving all life toward new heights of self-achievement and self-fulfillment.

The Purgatory Hypothesis

There is another concept that, though rarely examined in reincarnationist literature, is a valid one to consider: namely that, during this in-between state, the soul may make some effort to "purge" an especially angry or violent personality of the darkness that resides within it. This would not be unlike the Catholic concept of purgatory—a place of temporary punishment from which the victim is eventually rescued—except in this case it is intended as a place of spiritual refinement and teaching rather than as a place of punishment.

How might this work? Let's go back to our Nazi analogy for an example: imagine that, upon his death, the commandant of a Nazi death camp found himself inside his own camp as a prisoner, where he is subjected to all the humiliations, horrors, and terrors that he had so casually inflicted upon his prisoners when on Earth. It is all entirely illusory, of course, and is entirely orchestrated by the very soul that birthed the twisted personality, but it would seem very real to the personality living through it. So real would this imaginary world be, in fact, that the personality would imagine itself to be experiencing genuine physical and emotional suffering as part of the illusion, further demonstrating the ability of the mind to create a realistic Hell for itself where none, at least in the realm of the absolute, truly exists.

While I recognize this may sound punitive in nature, it is not designed as such. Instead, it is intended to be instructive, for it is through this process that the personality comes to appreciate the enormity of the evil it caused and, after a time, even comes to repent of it. In this way, the personality is effectively purged of the bile that held it hostage while on Earth, making its transition and reabsorption back into the higher self (the soul) ultimately possible. In fact, without this experience it may be impossible for the personality to be drawn back into the soul at all, for it may be so sick that it cannot endure the light of love and will thus be repelled by its own soul, making this purging process—as difficult and even at times painful as it is—absolutely necessary for integration to be possible. I imagine this would especially have applications for the criminally insane and other personalities that have strayed too far from the light of the soul that birthed them to find their way back.

Obviously, this is all purely speculative, but it does provide some possibilities with regard to what becomes of evil once it encounters the light of divine love. It may survive for a time, perhaps, to writhe in an agony of its own creation, but in the end I wouldn't be surprised if it isn't finally healed and brought back into the light, where it can at last move forward with the maturation process once again—the lessons it is required to learn being appreciated, if not on Earth during its lifetime, then in the realm of spirit after its death.

Of course, no one leaves the earth plane spiritually pure. We all carry prejudices, angers, regrets, and a whole suitcase of other negative feelings and attitudes into the spiritual realm when we make our transition, but I suspect most of that is burned away fairly quickly and the average person enters into the light fairly effortlessly, making the necessity of undergoing a type of purging process as I just described unnecessary. However, for those who may be so emotionally and spiritually corrupt as to make that transition impossible, it's nice to imagine that a process may be in place that deals with such poor individuals.

The Question of Ghosts

Before leaving the topic of the transition process from one incarnation to another, there is one more issue that frequently crops up: the question of ghosts. If the human personality, upon death, reintegrates back into the soul that birthed it (or potentially endures a type of purging process before doing so), what are we to do with the concept of ghosts? After all, ghosts—presuming one believes in such things—

are the manifestations of human consciousness trapped within the earth plane, but how can they be a part of the physical realm if they are supposed to be undergoing a life review or purging process? Some have even seriously suggested that the existence of ghosts constitutes evidence that reincarnation cannot be true, for if we reincarnate how can we also manifest as ghosts?

While there are several possibilities, I suspect the answer lies in the idea that there may well be a period of time—even a very lengthy period of time—during which the recently departed have the opportunity to "acclimate" to their disembodied existence, a time when one gets used to the idea of moving from the physical realm governed by the laws of time and space into the realm of spirit in which both time and space are nonexistent. This is done so as not to "shock" the personality by changing its environment too dramatically or suddenly (somewhat like jumping into a pool of ice-cold water after emerging from a sauna), therefore affording it an opportunity to transition at its own rate.

While in this "transition zone" between the two realms, however, the personality is effectively stuck with one foot in two worlds; existing as a noncorporeal entity on the one hand while still being governed to some degree by time and space (which is why ghosts are frequently "grounded" in one locale or another for a limited amount of time). Most people make their way through this transitory period fairly rapidly and move on to the spiritual realm, but unfortunately some do not. Some may be so attached to a physical locale (home, place of work, etc.) or to family and friends that they are reluctant to break those ties—even for their own good—while others may have suffered such sudden or unexpected deaths that they are too traumatized initially to accept that they have ended their earthly existence and move on. (Credible stories of ghosts often involve people who die violently or unexpectedly.) Such personalities, then, may in fact linger for some time on the periphery of the physical realm and acquire the title of "ghost" or "spirit." However, I think it is significant that hauntings rarely last more than a few decades at most, suggesting that even these "wandering souls" eventually find their way to the light and ultimately into the flesh once again.

Suicide and Euthanasia

One area that has been a frequent source of anguish and confusion among reincarnationists is that of how—and whether—suicide and euthanasia impact the process of rebirth. While this too is an area ripe for debate and prone to considerable conjecture, my hope here is merely to provide you with some ideas to consider as you ponder one of the great moral dilemmas of human nature—especially as it relates to the process of reincarnation.

Before we begin, however, it is necessary to clearly define our terms here. I differentiate between suicide and euthanasia in that suicide is driven primarily by emotional and psychological factors (guilt, depression, loneliness, fear of punishment, etc.), while euthanasia is driven primarily by physiological considerations (terminal illness, quality of life, mental incapacity, etc.). Their motivations are entirely different, and so they need to be examined from different perspectives. First, we will deal with the issue of suicide.

It has been commonly taught that suicide incurs bad karma because, in cutting short an incarnation, one circumvents the growth process and in so doing retards the soul's spiritual development. However, much of the reason suicide (and, to a lesser degree, euthanasia) is singled out for karmic retribution has less to do with the supposed breaking of some universal taboo and more to do with society's discomfort with the concept of self-destruction in general. As is common to most religious beliefs, we tend to perceive such issues through the limited lens of our own biases and condemn those actions we personally consider wrong almost entirely on an emotional basis. The belief that one acquires negative karma for taking one's own life persists not because it is a greater crime than any other, but because we collectively find our own premeditated self-destruction to be the most frightening act a human being can engage in, and it is those things we fear the most that we want to punish the most. As such, suicide is often singled out for special punishment, whereas "lesser crimes" might be simply dismissed as the naïve errors of a young and ignorant soul.

The reason suicide incurs such negative connotations is because it suggests we have tampered with the divine machinery of spiritual growth by ending an incarnation before its time. However, since we have no way of knowing from the context of the physical realm when a life is "supposed" to end, death at one's own hand is no more indicative of a circumvented incarnation than is one's accidental death in a plane crash. In effect, from the context of eternity there may be no "proper" time to die—when we do so is simply an element of our environment, our decision-making processes, and the vagaries of fate.

Clearly, the morality behind suicide is largely determined by a culture's own level of spiritual development and the impact its religious beliefs have on its moral values. We live in a society that fears death and therefore considers dying an enemy that must be staved off at all costs. Yet from the standpoint of eternity—where the soul is indestructible and immortal—death is not only effectively harmless but even unimportant. How and when one dies then is far less significant than what spiritual lessons the soul learned during that incarnation. Suicide may or may not be the sign of an immature soul, but regardless it has no impact on the soul's essential nature or state.

Of course, that's not to say a suicide won't have negative effects, particularly on those left behind. Guilt and anger are often a lasting legacy suicide leaves in its wake, but even then such experiences are nothing if not a part of the process of spiritual evolution. We are on this planet to realize a wide range of emotions and experiences—both positive and negative—of which the loss of loved ones, whether by natural causes or through an accident or even via suicide, is a part of the mix. We can't expect only to experience the good and be surprised and shocked when we also experience the bad. They both are necessary to realize the fullest effects of the process.

As for a person who takes his or her own life, the soul that inhabits that body is not acquiring bad karma but is simply moving through the process of spiritual growth from the perspective of its own level of understanding. The life review will examine the reasons it felt it necessary to end that particular incarnation and recognize what elements were active in bringing it to a point of such desperation. There may be some residual trauma that emerges in the next incarnation to deal with as a result, but in the end it will eventually be worked through.[13]

As far as assisted suicide or euthanasia go, the same situation still applies. The soul is not harmed by choosing to end its own suffering (though it may not acquire the full benefits from choosing to experience suffering as part of the process of becoming more aware), nor has it done anything wrong for doing so. The notion that only God has the right to terminate a life is nonsense; if that were the case we should never be able to perform an abortion, fight a war, execute a criminal, or even take a life in self-defense. In fact, we could extend this argument further and assume that since God has the ultimate say in whether we live or die, we would be equally wrong to circumvent "His will" by prolonging and preserving life. To remain logically consistent, we should not attempt to cure a child of leukemia or perform open-heart surgery lest we be taking events entirely out of God's hands and thus circumventing "His perfect will." Obviously, trying to determine God's will is a fool's game, and one riddled with fallacies and a marked lack of logic.

Reincarnation, in contrast, works from the premise that each of us is the captain of our soul and largely responsible for what happens to us. The decision to take our own life, then, must be one option always open to us, if only so we may truly remain utterly free to de-

---

13. Additionally, if reincarnation is a fact, then I suspect we may all have a few suicides on our spiritual résumé to contend with, so one would be wise not to judge others too harshly for taking their own life.

cide not to do it. Anything else restricts the growth process by limiting our choices and so renders the entire process moot. Whether we run aground through our own foolishness or run a good race, it must be primarily our decisions that get us there—which is precisely as it must be if we are ever to mature spiritually.

Conclusions

Trying to gauge what occurs in the interval between incarnations is a highly speculative exercise and one open to many interpretations, but I suspect there is more to the process than we can begin to imagine from our extremely limited perspective here in the physical realm. Certainly *something* has to occur after one incarnation is finished and before the next is embarked upon in order for the lessons acquired in the one to have an impact on the other. The personality that we perceive this world through is a thing of the physical realm, while the soul that births each personality is a creature of the spiritual realm, so it seems a near certainty that some sort of "merging" needs to take place at some point for any of it to make sense. I could be wrong about that, of course, but if so, I am unable to understand how the process might be capable of moving forward otherwise.

chapter thirteen

Choosing the Next Incarnation

One question that appears to be seldom discussed within reincarnationist literature is the issue of how the soul might choose the next "venue" within which to incarnate—an issue ripe with all sorts of possibilities and one that we need to consider if we are to understand how reincarnation works in its entirety.

How the soul goes about choosing its next incarnation is probably a matter of how mature the soul is. In Dr. Michael Newton's book *Journey of Souls: Case Studies of Life Between Lives*, he seems to suggest that often the next incarnation appears to be coolly and carefully planned to take advantage of the potential opportunities for growth the next life might promise. For some souls the process appears more chaotic, with younger souls choosing hastily or even reluctantly—like a schoolboy required to do his lessons when he'd rather be outside playing—which I consider to be consistent with human nature in general. Of course, neither process is better from the perspective of eternity, for each is simply a reflection of the maturity level of the individual soul.

To what degree the soul is capable of planning out the next incarnation is a matter of debate, however. Some believe every event of the next life is carefully scripted, with every significant detail being essentially preordained before the soul enters the fetus, while others see each life as a series of free-will decisions that may supersede any pre-birth planning. Still others see an apparent randomness about each new life, as though it were a roll of the dice with the results being driven more by good fortune than good planning (a prospect we discussed earlier in the chapter on karma). Yet if we are to use our own experiences in this present life as a guide, it seems all three camps may have something to contribute to the debate.

What I'm suggesting is that just as in this life we preplan events, change our minds at the last minute, and sometimes fall victim to forces beyond our control, the soul may operate in much the same way. It may be able to choose a particular venue into which to incarnate, but it may not be able to plan out an entire incarnation in precise detail due to circumstances beyond its control and the result of decisions it will make while in the flesh. In other words, the process appears to be carefully planned, subject to change without notice, and apparently affected by factors completely outside the soul's control— *all at the same time.*

While this may appear on the surface to be contradictory, it perfectly mirrors life in general. Just as in life we make plans, only to see them either come to perfect fruition or fall apart completely, so too within the spiritual realm we may well select a venue for our next incarnation—say, a specific gender, nationality, or social class—and even a general time frame into which we will be born. This especially makes sense if we work from the premise that the human soul possesses the same degree of free will in the spiritual realm as humans in the flesh do, in which case the argument can be made that we should have a good deal to say about where we end up next. The soul, after all, is a creative "machine" that is, at its very core, utterly and completely free. Even when it is in the flesh, it manages to possess a considerable amount of free will, often even within the confines of a restrictive society. Are we to imagine this capability ends at death? Additionally, having access to all the cosmic knowledge of the universe may give us an especially ideal perspective from which to choose our next set of parents or even a specific family to be born into (assuming a developing fetus is available). We could gauge from our perch outside of time precisely what sort of circumstances we might find ourselves in, as well as the potential for growth that such a set of circumstances might afford.

On the other hand, the soul may be content to simply let the "chips fall where they may" and take advantage of whatever circumstances it finds itself born into, yet even that decision—the decision *not* to make any specific plans—is itself a free-will choice. In either case, however, any planning the soul may do will take it only so far. Once it returns to physicality, it will again be able to choose the various paths it will take, each of which will open new doors while shutting others. As such, over time the course it takes may—especially in younger souls—become increasingly at variance with the original plan, to the point that any prior planning the soul may have done is eventually rendered moot. Other events may also intervene in the process, such as a war or natural disaster, that could impact the course of events and completely supersede any previous soul-planning that may have been done. In effect, one may shoot an arrow into the sky and aim it precisely where one will, but once it leaves the bow it is at the mercy of wind and gravity and a host of other factors that will ultimately determine where it finally lands. In the same way, then, the soul may send the personality into the world with certain goals or intentions in mind, but where it ends up is anyone's guess.

But shouldn't the soul "see" the future from the spiritual realm, and therefore design its next incarnation around whatever external incidents are slated to occur within the venue the soul has chosen? In other words, wouldn't the soul *know* it was going to be born as a man who would one day be drafted into the military and die on a foreign battlefield before any significant "soul work" could be accomplished, and simply change the venue?

While theoretically this makes sense, it fails to take into account that in order for the soul to realize the full range of human experience, it is imperative it *not* know what is going to happen next. Just as a novel is not as easily enjoyed if the ending has been learned beforehand, so too would the lessons obtained in each incarnation be voided if the soul anticipated them beforehand. The not knowing what is going to happen next is as important a part of the process as is choosing the next venue. In essence, the soul may be just as surprised about what happens as is the personality it manifests, which is precisely the way it must be for the process to have any meaning.

To better illustrate this point, imagine how bland life would be if you knew beforehand precisely how every decision you make is going to turn out. Imagine if you *knew* beforehand the contents of every Christmas present you opened—not *hoped* you knew what was inside each wrapped box or *prayed* you were getting what you'd asked for, but if you already *foresaw* each gift—how exciting would that be? Perhaps at first, the thought of getting a great gift makes this foresight seem unimportant, but a moment's consideration will demonstrate the grayness life would take on if we foresaw how everything was going to come out beforehand. Further, imagine if you knew beforehand that a business venture you were planning was going to end in failure and bankruptcy, but since it was preordained you had no choice but to go through with your doomed plans. How would you feel about life in general, knowing that failure was assured and financial ruin was all you had to look forward to? Surprise, relief, excitement, and feelings of elation and exuberance would not be possible if the outcome were always assured. It's the uncertainties of life that make life worth living—no matter how excruciatingly frustrating those uncertainties may sometimes prove to be.

As such, we cannot blithely assume the soul knows precisely what's going to happen in its next incarnation, making it possible for even the most carefully planned venue to fall apart or be circumvented by any number of factors. This doesn't mean the process has failed in the sense we normally think of the word, for growth of a kind—even if only in the short term—may have still occurred; it's only that the soul did not realize the greatest "bang for its buck" in this particular incarnation.

However, it should be recognized that the success of an incarnation is not measured by the longevity or range of experiences the soul's personality realized; it is entirely conceivable a soul may have a very limited agenda in mind for a particular incarnation and so dies young or achieves very little (by worldly standards) yet has still managed to achieve each of its primary goals completely. It's impossible to know what a soul's agenda is from our side of eternity and, as such, it's entirely possible a child who dies in infancy or a man who has worked a long, unextraordinary life in a coal mine may have fulfilled his soul's agenda perfectly, even if we may not be able to see how.

Finally, the ability to plan the venue of the next incarnation may be purely voluntary as well and, perhaps, not taken advantage of by very immature souls intent only on continuing their adventures in the flesh. As such, those lesser-developed souls—those that we refer to as "young souls"—may put little thought into their next incarnation, simply choosing instead to inhabit the first available fetus they happen upon. Just as young adults who make important life decisions with little forethought frequently end up in difficult situations, so too may these immature souls end up in extremely trying and difficult incarnations. In choosing their next fetus in haste, they may find themselves in the body of a crack-addicted infant or trapped within the prison of a child born into a near-vegetative state. This lack of prior planning may explain why some souls end up in such horrific incarnations; careful planning and wisdom are needed as much in the spiritual realm as they are in the physical.

Yet there is nothing wrong with choosing a venue hastily. Just as there is nothing that requires a person to plan out their life in intricate detail, so too may some souls be content to "go with the flow" and land wherever fate takes them, completely unconcerned about pursuing any particular agenda at all. They have all eternity, after all, to mature, and so there may be no particular need to rush the process. Even the most immature children usually grow up and eventually become responsible adults; it seems likely it is no different in the spiritual realm.

On the other hand, some very mature souls—realizing that all incarnations lead to some degree of growth—may also be content to travel down whatever road they find themselves and so decide against making any specific plans. Like the old man who chooses to walk the breadth of America with nothing more than a walking stick and his dog along for company, so too may old souls occasionally enjoy living by their wits and taking on an entirely spontaneous incarnation. There is, after all, a certain freedom in not being tied to a single plan of action but instead experiencing a day-to-day world completely free of deadlines or schedules.

For those of us somewhere in between, however, a preincarnate agenda might well be in order and some careful planning done—at least on a superficial level. Most of us are not comfortable enough to perform "without a net" and may want some blueprints to follow, and so we may well have opportunities to craft them. How much choice we have in putting our plans together, however, may depend entirely on our needs and level of spiritual development. It may also be that along with greater spiritual maturity comes greater choice. Just as is true of maturity in general, once one becomes a more responsible decision-maker, the opportunities to make increasingly significant decisions increase as well.

Cultural Influences on a New Incarnation

It's not only possible but entirely likely that culture may play a role in this process as well. Reincarnationist researcher Dr. Ian Stevenson frequently noted that many of his subjects recalled having lived their previous life in very close proximity to their current place of residence; among the Tlingit Indians of Alaska—one of the Native American tribes that incorporate strong reincarnationist beliefs into their culture—Stevenson noted that sometimes the deceased soul appeared to return to the same tribe or even family. Reincarnation in these cases also tended to take place much faster than the norm, with intervals of as little as eight to ten months between death and rebirth (as compared to a more common average of around thirty years). All of this suggests a great deal of choice in the reincarnation process as well as a tendency for the soul to so closely identify with a particular culture that it tends to return to that culture (or a similar one) repeatedly, thereby severely limiting its range of potential experiences. As such, it might be argued that this is indicative of souls that were still either very young or so thoroughly identified with a specific place or culture as to be uncomfortable moving outside of it, effectively confining them to a repeating venue. This, however, doesn't mean that spiritual evolution or maturation isn't still taking place on some level. Reincarnation is a patient process that is in no rush to achieve its ultimate goal, so a soul that insists on spending numerous lifetimes locked into a familiar and comfortable locale or social venue is not doing anything wrong. It is simply experiencing life at the level of its development; when it is ready, it may finally move on to more fruitful pursuits and the process will continue.

On the other hand, an "older" soul may also choose to repeat similar venues because it is trying to accomplish some specific task that may be possible only within the context of a specific culture. It may even have a particular affinity for a specific culture or a mission it feels compelled to accomplish within that culture, resulting in repeated incarnations into the same venue. An example of this might be a soul that is intent on bringing enlightenment to the people of China and so continually reincarnates as a holy man within that nation over a period of many centuries. (Even the Bible seems to imply this idea with the suggestion by some in the Gospels that Jesus of Nazareth was a manifestation of the Old Testament prophet Elijah, implying that the soul that crafted Jesus had emerged into the Jewish culture more than once.)

As a rule, however, it is likely that more mature souls attempt to experience a range of different venues and so put more thought into the next incarnation. That's not to say they automatically select "easier" incarnations—or, for that matter, "harder" incarnations (which are subjective terms in any case)—but rather that they will choose an incarnation that will put them into a situation where the chances for positive spiritual growth are maximized. The soul could still select poorly, of course, but the selection process itself may still be far more deliberate than that shown by a younger, less mature soul. Yet the wisest person still occasionally makes a mistake, so the process of rebirth has an element of randomness and, if one wishes, even "luck" involved, even with the most seasoned souls.

Returning as an Animal?

One question that has been repeatedly asked of me when I present seminars on reincarnation is whether animals can reincarnate, and if we might reincarnate as animals ourselves. The idea that animals reincarnate or, more precisely, that we can reincarnate as an animal, is known technically as *transmigration*, and is normally taught—at least in the East—as the consequence of acquiring too much "bad" karma, resulting in an especially wicked person returning as an animal or some lesser creature such as an insect. Some even maintain that one might come back as a plant or, in an extreme case, a stone or some other inanimate object. (While this sounds almost incredulous, it must be remembered that the Eastern mind accepts that *all* things—even inanimate objects—possess souls, and so it's no more difficult to imagine that one might inhabit a rock than it would be to inhabit an ox.)

Transmigration is thought to be the ultimate humiliation for the soul, for in binding it to a "lowly" creature, it is forced to endure a brutal and short life with little hope for redemption or opportunity to be reborn back into human form. It works from the premise that no matter how difficult a human life might be, even the most wretched of them is better than living out an incarnation as a "mere" animal—

especially one of the lower creatures. In some traditions, this concept is so completely entrenched in the cultural psyche that every effort is made to avoid killing animals; in extreme cases, believers will actually sweep the path in front of them with a small broom in an effort to keep from inadvertently stepping upon an insect, lest they come back themselves as an insect as retribution for their negligence.

While I can respect anyone's beliefs, I believe the idea of transmigration has several serious problems inherent to it. First, it fails to explain how a soul might gain anything spiritually if it is born into a creature that does not possess sentience. A sense of self-awareness and a moral nature would seem to be the minimal prerequisite required in order to appreciate any spiritual growth, yet if the purpose of a lower incarnation is to induce the soul toward a higher level of consciousness, how is this to be realized within the tiny brain of a rat? As such, there seems to be no upward mechanism by which the soul might move toward spiritual maturity from within the context of transmigration, since animals are amoral creatures incapable of being either good or bad.

Second, it assumes life as an animal is a worse fate than life as a human, but this is debatable. Certainly it seems that some animals live a fairly carefree existence, and in the case of some birds or jungle predators (not to mention house pets) their lives might even be considered idyllic. Has one never fantasized what it would be to fly free like an eagle or be a powerful lion spending one's days hunting gazelle through lush grasslands? If not, why do such terms as "it's a dog's life" or "free as a bird" possess such positive connotations?

Third, most animals have life spans that are far shorter than that of a human being, making an incarnation as an animal—assuming it is done as a punishment—far more short-term and, as a result, less punitive. It could be argued that a long life as a man or woman might not only be more difficult than that of an animal, but as it would last longer it would make a human incarnation a much more effective and difficult punishment and thus a far better tool for rendering justice, if justice were the real issue here.

As such, it seems that transmigration of the soul is a far poorer mechanism for extracting either justice or teaching spiritual lessons than traditional reincarnation. If the purpose of the soul is spiritual maturity, then incarnating into the body of an animal would appear to be a step in the wrong direction and utterly detrimental to what the rebirthing process is trying to accomplish. Except for those rare cases where a person might purposely enter into the body of an animal for some religious or symbolic reason,[14] it's difficult to see how transmigration would be of any use.

Considering an Alien Venue

While returning as an animal would be, in my opinion, counterproductive to spiritual maturation, that does not preclude the possibility that a soul may generate nonhuman yet still conscious personalities on other planets. In effect, we can't assume that the soul is always going to reincarnate back on Earth; it way well find other venues elsewhere in the cosmos where it might grow equally as well.

However, this premise does have one caveat attached to it: according to many past-life therapists, it is exceedingly rare to find a subject who recalls having lived on another planet in a past life (although people recalling having lived on Atlantis is not unheard of), which suggests that intelligent life resides only on this single planet, with Earth being the lone beacon of life among an ocean of stars. This seems rather unlikely, however, especially considering the vastness of not only our own galaxy but also the fact that there are literally billions of other galaxies much like our own strung out across the expanse of the universe. Yet if life is ubiquitous, then why are there so few memories of people having lived as, say, an intelligent slug on the shores of the ammonia seas on Rigel's fourth planet? It seems being

---

14. Such teachings can sometimes be found within the traditions of the Native American religions, though even then such human-to-animal transitions are rare.

continually reincarnated onto this single planet should be most limiting and even have the potential of restricting a soul's potential for growth by confining it to this single earthly venue. As such, if it is the soul's goal to experience life on many levels, why are no extraterrestrial pasts thrown in to the mix?

While several possibilities present themselves, the simplest answer is that the soul chooses to stay within the confines of what it knows best, restricting itself to a single venue through countless incarnations until it has learned all there is to learn there. This would make sense, especially from a soul-growth perspective, for that would permit the soul to continue its growth unimpeded by the need to thoroughly readjust itself to a new physical reality each time it reincarnates.

Consider the likelihood that the universe is home to millions of species of sentient creatures, each of which exists within its own unique and distinct environment and culture. One creature may be completely aquatic and make its home at extreme ocean depths while another may do nicely floating like a blimp through a pure methane atmosphere. One may find temperatures of several hundred degrees Fahrenheit most comfortable while another prefers a temperature only a few degrees above absolute zero. And culturally, they may possess an even more exotic and alien psyche, one so unlike our own as to make any similarities between us and them purely coincidental. As such, to move from one of these truly alien environments onto Earth would not only be to take on a new body, but an entirely new mindset as well. If the traumas of a past life can come back to haunt us in our current incarnation, imagine how much more so a past life as an insect-like being that spent its days writing poetry and devouring smaller bugs might affect our current perceptions. In essence, it may be more than the soul can handle, making a return to a similar venue more desirable and probably far less traumatic.

Of course, there may be alien beings much like ourselves out there as well, but even if we shared a similar physiology with our extraterrestrial cousins, it's unlikely we would share a similar culture, history, mentality, or morality, making an incarnation on Earth still largely problematic. While we may one day leave the earth plane completely and move on to an entirely new venue (in fact, we may well be forced to once life becomes unsustainable on this planet), it seems logical to assume that when that happens, it will be more of a mass exodus than a gradual migration. Our reincarnating on this planet works for us because we've become acclimated to it. In effect, we stay here for the simple reason that we "understand the rules" of Earth via the many lifetimes lived here and so find reincarnating here more efficient and effective. To do otherwise would be the equivalent of changing universities at the end of each semester; having to learn a new campus with new instructors and even new standards couldn't help but set us back scholastically. To stay at the "University of Earth" throughout the entire education process makes the learning process far less problematic in that each semester builds upon the previous one, affording us an unbroken progression through which we might more easily advance through our studies.

Then again, it's entirely possible some of us have lived on other planets before (I've met a few people in my lifetime I've suspected of this), but we simply don't retain the memory of having done so. Just as it seems we are better able to recall our last incarnation than the one that preceded it, so it is possible that if we go back far enough, the memories of having lived in an alien world might well have evaporated. In the same way, perhaps one day our memories of having lived on this planet will similarly fade by the third or fourth incarnation on another world thousands of light years away.

It's also possible that due to the dramatic differences we experience when moving from one physical world into another, our soul simply expunges such memories from our subconscious, making them entirely unreachable to even the best past-life regression therapist. Perhaps there's a built-in "safety mechanism" designed specifically to prevent us from being too traumatized when a new incarnation is more than our psyche can handle. Or maybe our past on another planet is so alien to our current personality—which is, after all, filtering past-life memories through its modern understanding—that it simply ignores those memories it can't relate to. As humans, we understand what it is to have been a human in a past life, but as we have no context within which to understand a past incarnation on an alien world, we may ignore those memories entirely, much like a child will ignore a complex algebraic equation written on a chalkboard because it's too complex for his or her undeveloped mind to fathom.

Finally, there is the possibility that as we mature spiritually and become more capable of grasping the nuances and complexities of an alien mindset, we may eventually develop a greater capacity to recall past lives lived on alien worlds. Additionally, some souls may be ready for the challenge another physical existence could provide and thus choose to leave the earth plane entirely and sample some "alien cuisine," with all the challenges and opportunities for growth such a world might offer. The universe is, after all, a very big place, and we have all eternity to play out a billion different dramas if we so wish.

Conclusions

It should be apparent that the process of rebirth is a complex and sophisticated one that takes into account a myriad of factors beyond our comprehension. Just as no good drama is possible without significant planning behind the scenes, so too does the process of choosing our next incarnation become an important one. It may appear in some ways to be beyond our understanding, but it is a process that works to perfection in helping us realize the divinity that resides within us. It may appear hopelessly complex, but it is this complexity that makes it such a superior tool for spiritual growth, for it takes everything into account and leaves nothing out. Even those elements that may appear at first glance to be random are figured in to the mix, making it a perfect mechanism for spiritual evolution.

Therefore the question of what happens to us between incarnations and, especially, the question of whether there is a judgment of some kind should not fill us with trepidation and fear, but should be approached with confidence that the process not only knows what it's doing, but also that it is compassionate and kind in carrying it out. It is not the process we need to fear, but rather it is our own doubts about God and His compassion and eternal love that we need to confront and vanquish if we are to realize the fullness and richness each individual incarnation affords us on a daily basis.

chapter fourteen

Coming Into the Flesh

The question of precisely when a soul enters the fetus—in essence, the moment life begins—is not only an interesting philosophical question but also an emotional and moral one, replete with significant religious and even political overtones. As such, having looked at the process of rebirth from the planning stage in some detail, it might be helpful to look at the mechanics involved in returning to the earth plane. This process is important, since it relates to questions having to do with birth control, abortion, euthanasia, and what is going on with miscarriages and stillborns. While I can offer no firm and fast rules on any of these issues, I can offer a few observations and no small amount of speculation in the hope that some readers may find in these theories reassurance about the process.

The Start of the Process

Perhaps the most common presumption made by reincarnationists and traditionalists alike is that the soul enters the fetus upon conception. However, this is by no means self-evident nor is it the only position possible. In fact, the prospect that a successfully conceived egg or a three-day old embryo is endowed with a soul can only be presumed, for there is no medical means by which this might be determined. Of course, since there is no scientific means to demonstrate that an infant—or an adult, for that matter—possesses a soul, the argument must, by necessity, remain an element of faith.

However, from the perspective of reincarnation, I submit that the precise moment at which a soul enters a developing fetus is of only minor concern. While some reincarnationists do teach that the soul enters at the precise second of conception, I suspect this may be more of a politically or religiously popular belief rather than a logical one, especially if we work from the premise that most souls plan their next incarnation (at least to some degree)—in which case indwelling a fertilized egg instantly may not only prove premature but potentially even a waste of time.

What if the embryo proves to be nonviable, resulting in a miscarriage? What if it is aborted, or is stillborn (a question we will examine in more detail in a moment), or has a severe birth defect that will prevent the soul that indwells the embryo from living out its planned path in the next incarnation? I suppose it's possible from the perspective of eternity that the higher self may know the answers to these questions beforehand (precognizance), but if that's the case, it would argue against the idea that all embryos have souls upon conception—for what soul would make the decision to indwell an embryo it knew was not going to be viable or was slated for destruction?

As such, we are left with a choice to make: either the soul knows an embryo is not viable and agrees to indwell it anyway—even if only for a few days until it is expelled from the uterine walls—or it doesn't know beforehand the precise fate of an embryo and effectively waits until it finds one that is firmly affixed to the uterine wall before indwelling it, which would make an embryo "soulish" at the point of viability rather than at the moment of conception. Further, there is the genetics issue to take into account. Might the soul wait to determine not only the embryo's viability but also its genetic makeup, as well as other factors such as the health of the mother (drug dependency?) or the likelihood of being aborted, before "committing" to the embryo?

In that case, the fetus may choose not to inhabit a soul until much later in the gestation period or, potentially, even until the actual moment of birth itself.[15]

It is not unreasonable to imagine that souls may "seek out" a fetus to indwell in much the same way that a bird searches diligently for a tree within which to build its nest. The bird doesn't construct its nest within the thin branches of a sapling but looks instead for a tree of sufficient maturity and size to support not only the weight of the bird and its nest but one also capable of providing shelter from the wind and rain. In the same way, then, the idea that a soul seeks out a fetus at a more mature stage of development rather than a recently fertilized embryo makes sense, for such would allow the soul to determine the viability of the developing fetus and whether it had any inherent birth defects that might prove detrimental (or, for that matter, beneficial) to its spiritual agenda, as well as determine its parentage, nationality, gender, and so on. Then, once it has determined the fetus to be both viable and in alignment with its wishes, the soul enters the fetus—either incrementally and progressively[16] or, perhaps, all at once—to wait out its traumatic birth as well as to give the soul time to readjust to the world of linear time and space once again.

When this might be is a guess, of course, but since infants regularly survive premature birth and grow up with an apparently intact soul, it would seem reasonable to assume the soul enters the fetus at some point immediately before a prematurely born fetus might survive outside the womb (roughly speaking, late in the second trimester[17]). It's

---

15. This position has been suggested by some astrologers, which is why one's precise moment and date of birth determines their destiny—the assumption being that the soul entered the fetus at that precise moment rather than at some earlier point.

16. Though the personality is a byproduct of the soul, it exists within the physical mechanism of the brain, suggesting that perhaps the personality "grows" with the brain, becoming more fully formed as the brain that houses it also grows more fully formed and, as such, capable of "holding" the personality.

17. In some parlances, this is known as the point of "quickening."

possible some souls enter earlier and some much later (almost imme-diately before birth), but a time frame of late in the second trimester seems reasonable from the standpoint of viability and logic.

This, however, brings up several interesting questions. For example, can a soul occupy and then abandon a fetus before birth or, even more intriguing, is it possible for a person to be born without a resident soul at all? And, is it possible for more than one soul to claim the same fetus? In effect, might souls actually contend for the right to occupy a particularly "choice" fetus? And what about identical twins? Are we looking at a single soul that has split, or is it a case of a single soul occupying two different bodies simultaneously? While none of these answers can be known with any certainty, we can hazard a few guesses that might shine some light on these questions.

First, in terms of whether a fetus might conceivably be born with-out a resident soul, it is difficult to imagine how a personality could exist apart from a soul, especially if we assume the personality to be an outgrowth or reflection of the soul. Though it's possible a soul might not enter until days or even mere hours before birth (some have even alluded to the possibility that souls could enter shortly *after* birth), if a fetus failed to acquire a soul prior to—or immediately after—birth, it is hard to imagine how the fetus might survive. Could this be what happens to those fully formed and apparently viable fetuses that are stillborn? It's an intriguing possibility.

As for whether a soul might abandon a developing fetus, this may be possible but, if it does occur, I'd imagine it to be exceedingly rare. As the fetus is developing in the womb, once the soul takes up resi-dence within the body it effectively grows and expands within the developing infant, becoming larger and more fully realized as time passes. To remove itself from the body at this point might not only be difficult, but even painful to the soul—making it more probable it would choose to stay with its chosen host rather than abandon the project and look elsewhere for another fetus. It is, in effect, committed to the incarnation and can only be pulled away from it in the case of a miscarriage or abortion.

However, while it's probably rare, there is no particularly compelling reason why a soul couldn't change its mind even while in the spiritual realm—just as the personality it births frequently can and does in the physical realm—and so decide to abandon a viable fetus of its own accord. Why a soul would choose to do such a thing remains enigmatic—perhaps it is an extremely immature soul that chose in great haste and decided it was coming into an especially difficult incarnation it was not ready to deal with—but it has to be considered as a possibility.

On the other hand, abandoning a developing fetus may not necessarily be the decision of the soul but is determined—at least in part—by physiological factors. For example, a soul may take up residence in a fetus at an early stage only to discover the fetus is developing a congenital defect that will result in it being born into a severely mentally disabled or even vegetative state. If the soul decides that may prove detrimental to its spiritual development, it may choose to abandon the fetus entirely, resulting in a miscarriage (although it's also possible that just such a "defective" fetus may be precisely what a more advanced soul would require for its development; most likely, however, the average soul would probably opt to abandon the fetus and consider it a "false start"). It's also possible the decision to abandon the fetus may not be made by the soul, but by the fetus.[18] It's not unreasonable, for example, to imagine a fetus simply expelling its host soul once it became obvious it was not going to be viable, forcing the soul to seek out another host and effectively demonstrating how the physi-

---

18. Some may wonder how a fetus could make a decision as to whether it is inhabited or not, to which I respond that the fetus itself—being as much a part of the universe as the soul—may also possess a degree of consciousness, a kind of divine awareness with which it can communicate directly with the very soul that is attempting to indwell it. This is purely conjectural, I know, but it's consistent with the belief that all matter possesses a type of inherent consciousness, even if imperceptible to our senses.

cal and spiritual realms might work together in the quest for spiritual maturation.

Fighting Over Baby

The question of determining which soul gets which body is more problematic and, in my opinion, more intriguing. Certainly the idea of souls contending for some poor fetus like a pair of starving dogs fighting over an old bone is ludicrous, and I doubt the spiritual realm is quite as contentious as our physical world is, especially in regard to possessions. My guess is that there is some kind of "seniority" system in place in which more highly evolved souls get to select first, followed by lesser-evolved souls, with the youngest and most immature souls finally being allowed to pick over what's left. Perhaps some fetuses are specifically "tagged" for more advanced souls by spirit masters because of their potential value, while others are thought to hold such limited potential for significant growth that they are left for the younger souls. On the other hand, those fetuses being born into especially promising venues—spiritually speaking—might be set aside specifically for those younger souls who need maturing the most (with the assumption being that the older, more mature souls can do more with less). In either case, I imagine the process is a lot less messy in the spiritual realm than it would be if played out in the physical realm, though considering that there may be spiritually primitive souls involved, one can never be certain that the process would be any less chaotic in the realm of spirit than it is in the flesh.

The entire argument might be rendered moot, however, if we look at it from the perspective of eternity. No fetus may be considered better or worse or more promising or less promising than another; all may have—and probably do have—the same value in our maturing process. Each developing fetus provides a unique venue from which to experience life in all its many facets; it is up to the resident soul to decide what to do with that life. As such, a child born into great poverty might, in the end, prove to grow far more spiritually throughout its short, deprived life than had it been born into great wealth. It is the difficulties of life and our abilities to overcome them that gives birth to spiritual growth—not the time, place, and venue of our next incarnation.

The Multiple Personality Disorder Phenomenon

The prospect of souls "fighting" over a fetus may be as pointless an exercise as might be imagined, especially from the perspective of eternity. However, it does bring up some peripheral issues that need to be explored. For instance, is it possible for more than a single soul to occupy a particular fetus? We naturally assume we all have but a single soul and, as such, a single personality, but what if that is not always the case? Could multiple souls inhabiting a single body be one possible explanation for cases of multiple personality disorder (MPD)?

For those not familiar with this rare and debilitating condition, MPD is a psychological disorder in which a person exhibits more than one established, distinct personality (and may, in some rare cases, exhibit literally dozens of such personalities). What causes it is not entirely clear, but it seems to be a defense mechanism built in to the human psyche that causes the personality to split or "shatter" during times of tremendous stress or trauma—especially if such trauma is experienced early in childhood. In effect, the theory goes, in order to keep the psyche from complete disintegration, the personality breaks into smaller, compartmentalized parts (each of which apparently is safer from disintegration than a whole personality might be), resulting in numerous, often contradictory personalities emerging in later life. For example, one personality might be somber and restrained, while another is playful and vivacious; another might be sexually prudish, while still another exhibits itself as being promiscuous. Each is a part of the whole person, but since they are not integrated into a single seamless personality, they put the individual suffering from such a disorder in a difficult situation. This is especially true as many of the personalities are not aware of the existence of the others—resulting in frequently embarrassing situations that leave the primary personality at a loss for how it got into a particular fix it finds itself in. It is only with considerable work and patience on the part of a good therapist (and a tremendous willingness on the part of the victim) that these pieces of the greater personality can be successfully fused back together, restoring order to the sufferer's life.

So, what does this have to do with the idea of various souls contending for a developing fetus? Just the thought that in some cases of MPD, it is possible some of these competing personalities are not fragmented pieces of a greater personality, but—in exhibiting evidence of being complete, whole personalities in their own right—may be, in fact, "secondary" souls all inhabiting a single body.

Apparently many mental health professionals who deal with MPD patients note that some and, indeed, many of the personalities they encounter do not appear to be incomplete—as one would expect from a fractured element of a greater personality—but appear to be fully intact personalities that exhibit a complete range of emotions, their own unique physiology, and even distinct brain-wave patterns. For example, one personality may have a severe allergy to pollen while another does not; each may have different blood pressures and pulse rates; and one might even have better eyesight or hearing than another, even though they are all emanating from the same person. This leads one to conclude that either the brain has a remarkable and little-understood ability to dramatically affect the body's physiology, or there may be more than a single soul inhabiting one body (or perhaps, to some degree, both aspects are in play).

Is it possible that in some cases a fetus may genuinely be inhabited by more than one soul—say, either a series of primitive souls or a stronger primary soul and several younger souls along for the ride—and that these alter egos don't appear until and unless there is some trauma that brings them to the surface? In essence, our body might be hosting more than a single personality, but they remain hidden as long as our predominate personality remains intact—in effect "masking" each of the more primitive souls within the shadow of a larger, more dominant primary soul.

While this may sound fantastic, evidence for this theory might be contained within the tendency in some people toward sudden and dramatic mood swings. Probably everyone knows someone who appears energized and optimistic one moment and depressed and tired an hour later, irritable and angry on another occasion and patient and forgiving on another, and even intellectually sharp one moment and frightfully dull another. Could these moods, then, be not simply a single soul manifesting particular energies from moment to moment, but in fact be a series of personalities—some so subtle as to be almost indistinguishable—emerging under just the right conditions? Could these different energies we put off at different times be the subtle efforts of very young and primitive personalities to exert themselves? Even if they're not powerful enough to dramatically impact the primary personality, could they be strong enough to still influence it to some degree?

It's an intriguing possibility, and one that suggests that very immature souls may in effect "piggyback" onto more mature souls through an incarnation, much like an older, wiser sibling might take the hand of her baby brother in a crowd. It may be possible that some souls are too immature to take on a solo incarnation and need to be shown "the ropes" by more mature souls, and that as long as the host does not suffer the sort of trauma that results in the personality shattering, it will reside deep within the psyche of that person completely unnoticed throughout an entire lifetime. In this way, then, a very primitive soul may be able to learn simply by staying in the background and watching the more mature soul live out its incarnation and so be more prepared the next time around to "fly solo" in its own body.

This would have a number of benefits from the soul's perspective. First, it would be a way of effectively shepherding a primitive soul through the growth process instead of letting it take on an incarnation it's not mature enough to handle. Just as we don't let a teenager drive a car until he's had some time behind the wheel, perhaps the same might be true in the spiritual realm as well, with older, more mature souls in effect taking "junior along for a ride" to let them get the feel of how an incarnation operates. Then, when they are ready, the newer souls are given the keys, so to speak, and permitted to go it alone. This would also have the effect of limiting the mischief an underdeveloped soul could get into, making the older soul a type of baby-sitter or surrogate parent to the young soul. As long as the primitive soul is kept under control, the human host need never be aware of its presence and could live a lifetime entirely unaware he possessed a number of younger souls within his psyche.

Second, this would also be a means by which more mature souls might grow as well, for in setting examples for the younger soul, they may be learning a great deal themselves. Just as young men and women frequently mature much more quickly once they become parents, so too might it be that the maturing soul can make great leaps in its development if it serves in the role of teacher for a time. If we work from the premise that all souls are a manifestation of the Divine and at their heart are simply a part of a single larger soul, it makes sense there would be considerable cooperation among the various souls, all for their mutual benefit.

While a fantastic idea and probably an unnecessary appendage to understanding reincarnation, it would account for some of the more remarkable aspects of MPD as well as have something to say about "demonic" possession (which may not be the result of a demon at all, but simply a primitive and angry soul resisting being cast out of its host due to fear). Certainly, it answers some questions nicely, though admittedly it creates a host of new questions in the process.

The Prospect of Rogue Souls

One of the lesser-known paradoxes to deal with is the possibility that a particularly primitive soul might forcefully eject another soul from either a still-developing fetus or, conceivably, even from an already born human. While probably rare, it is something to consider and an important possibility to take a look at.

What brings the entire issue up are those rare cases Dr. Ian Stevenson encountered over the course of his studies of past-life memories in children, when it appeared that the previous-life personality the child recounted had died shortly *after* the child's own birth. In effect, young Hamid could recall a past life as Rajiv that is both credible and verifiable, only to later have it discovered that Rajiv did not die until nearly a year after Hamid was born. Of course, this should be utterly impossible if we are to imagine that incarnations are sequential, thus throwing the entire issue into doubt.

Admittedly this is one of the bigger puzzles about reincarnation, but, as we take a speculative look at how souls might contend for a developing fetus or even piggyback onto another soul, isn't it possible a "rogue" soul could decide to circumvent the rebirth process and simply seize an already occupied host body, effectively "claim jumping" by expelling the previous, weaker occupant—thus committing a form of spiritual thievery?

It might be imagined this is something that only the most brazen and immature soul might try, and it's difficult to imagine there wouldn't be certain safeguards in place specifically to prevent such a thing from happening, but we cannot be certain of that. Further, there's the possibility that a more mature soul might willingly surrender its host to another soul if it felt the younger soul might benefit from taking on that particular incarnation. How this works precisely can only be guessed at, but it suggests that the mechanics of the rebirth process may be far more complex and free-will driven than we can imagine. It may even be that the process of returning to the flesh lies well beyond our ability to understand at all, demanding instead that we simply learn to trust the process rather than try to comprehend it in all its complexity, which is probably the best advice of all.

The Question of Twins

Another interesting question within the realm of the mechanics of reincarnation is what to make of identical twins. That identical twins frequently share a significant number of personality traits is well documented, and while science explains this as the result of sharing the same genetic characteristics and similar environments, it fails to explain why such close parallels in personality are not as frequently found—or as pronounced—in fraternal twins as well, since they too are almost invariably raised under identical circumstances.[19] Further, there is the question of those rare sets of identical twins being separated at birth who reunite years later only to find they not only share many physical characteristics and temperament but even share similar tastes in clothing, hobbies, professions, and even mates. Colin Wilson cites two examples in his extensive work *Beyond the Occult*, in which he writes of two cases of separated twins whose lives seemed almost to mirror each other's, right down to suffering similar mishaps at the same ages, marrying spouses with the same name, and having an identical number of children!

This clearly seems to argue for at least a "soul mix" in identical twins, if not a single soul residing within two physical bodies. Yet it is hard to imagine how a single soul could manifest two nearly identical personalities simultaneously and be able to work through both, especially when they are separated by great distances. But then, we so poorly understand this process in any case that such may not only be possible but even common. The fact that a single soul can occupy two physical forms at the same time should be no more remarkable than the idea that it can occupy a single human form; within the context of eternity, any of this may be not only possible but entirely probable.

---

19. One possible explanation for this disparity may be that whereas identical twins come from a single fertilized egg that splits during the first few days of gestation, fraternal twins come from two separate eggs, thereby producing greater variation between the resultant personalities.

It is also possible there is such a thing as "complementary souls"—souls so close in temperament and personality as to be almost carbon copies of each other—that choose to travel together through multiple incarnations, always manifesting through sets of identical twins (or even triplets). Considering the almost unlimited combinations of soul and body experiences, it would not be far-fetched to imagine almost anything to be possible in the spiritual realm, right down to souls that travel like a pack of wolves—not in an effort to hunt down and destroy but in an effort to facilitate and participate in each other's spiritual evolution.

The mechanism of reincarnation is mysterious and it produces as many questions as answers; this could be one of the areas in which we are fated only to guess. While it would be nice to understand this process more fully, it probably is not necessary that we do so. Perhaps one day, once we attain a higher level of spiritual understanding both individually and collectively, we may be ready to tackle these questions, but for now we shall have to settle for mere speculation.

The Abortion Issue

Finally, there is the controversial and emotional question of abortion. Is it murder—especially if one decides that life begins at conception, thereby rendering all efforts to terminate a pregnancy at any point effectively an act of homicide—or does life begin at some later point in the process, perhaps at the moment of viability of the fetus (the point at which it would be capable of surviving outside the womb, usually at some point during the second trimester), which then makes an early-stage abortion a medical issue rather than a moral one? Finally, if one defines life as beginning at the moment the first breath is drawn, even late-term abortion is acceptable, making the question an important one to consider.

While the ethics and morality of aborting a viable fetus may be a hotly debated political and moral issue, the question is rarely asked about how this might affect the rebirth cycle. Does it throw the entire process off, or does it have little or no appreciable impact on the soul's quest to reenter into the flesh? And what becomes of the resident soul once the decision to abort is made? Is the soul destroyed along with the fetus, or does it continue on? Further, what responsibility does a soon-to-be mother have in this case? Is she acquiring "bad karma" for her decision to abort, or does it not make any difference?

Part of the answer may have to do with what point in the pregnancy the procedure was performed; if very early, the fetus may be unoccupied by a soul and so no real damage is done, making the procedure a purely medical issue rather than an ethical one (though it may still incur detrimental psychological/emotional effects for the mother later in life). If performed after the soul has taken up residency, however, an abortion would be the equivalent of destroying a bird's nest or obliterating a beehive: it would not destroy the soul, but it would force it to flee, possibly resulting in it taking up residency in another fetus that might prove less than ideal for it.

As for whether this might result in "bad karma" for the mother, the concept of karma—at least as generally understood in the West—is not a logical one. As such, the mother would not acquire *any* kind of negative repercussions for her decision in the spiritual realm; she may still have to deal with the natural consequences of her decision in the physical realm—guilt, remorse, and a diminished sense of self-esteem being the most frequent effects—but it would have no impact on her next incarnation (except, perhaps, as a residual memory that manifests itself as a strong desire for a child in a future incarnation). Additionally, if her decision to abort is a result of her own level of spiritual development, it would be illogical to punish her for simply acting within the context of her own level of spiritual maturity and understanding. The universe is nothing if not patient and forgiving.

Further, it is possible that a soul can anticipate the spiritual state of a mother and how likely she is to abort and thus delay joining with the fetus until after the decision not to abort is made. It is reasonable to imagine such knowledge is available to the spiritual realm, especially if one accepts the idea that each soul has spiritual mentors to guide it into the next incarnation. What's not known, of course, is how extensive this information might be and if these mentors can actually see into the future, or whether they simply make an educated guess based upon their knowledge of the level of maturity of the soul in residency within the mother. Perhaps it's a bit of both.

Conclusions

The mechanics of returning to physicality are complex and beyond our current understanding, and are likely to remain that way for the foreseeable future. Fortunately, however, it is not necessary we understand the process to appreciate it for its inherent perfection and ultimate value. We all have questions as to why some people are born with heartbreaking deformities or genetic proclivities toward cancer or heart disease, yet we only perceive the process from our very limited perspective on this side of eternity. Likely there are a great number of things going on simultaneously on many different fronts, each of them interrelated and co-joined to form a unique tapestry of life. They are mysteries we can only ponder and accept as a part of the process of spiritual growth.

We need only retain faith that the universe is a place of love and compassion to know that no matter what happens, everything will work out in the end. We may not always experience only joyous things—children and their mothers sometimes die in childbirth, and the occurrence of a miscarriage or stillborn birth is heart wrenching, but even so it is important to understand is that the Divine Spirit is still in charge and all is well. Even the tragedies of life can be beneficial down the road (even when we can't see it at the time), so trust the process and learn what you can learn from each disappointment, for it is within the challenges and tribulations of life that the spirit of God glows most brightly.

Life is not a place to fear but a spectacular experience to immerse oneself in. It is our playground of possibilities, the stage upon which we live out each act, and the venue within which God experiences Himself. What happens to us, whether in life or between lives, is in God's hands and we can rest assured that because of that we are safe, for God realizes that in dealing with each soul, He is dealing with the sacred.

chapter fifteen

The End Game

What finally happens when our soul finishes its journey? After it has come into the flesh countless times, either here on Earth or elsewhere in the cosmos, and has fulfilled its agenda, what happens to it? What more is there for it to do, to experience, once it has completed its quota of incarnations?

This is one of the most common questions I'm asked about the reincarnation process and, in some ways, it's one of the most difficult to answer. Some traditions—especially Eastern religious traditions—maintain that reincarnating never ends but goes on through eternity, manifesting one new personality after another in a never-ending process of enlightenment. To the Western mind, which is used to thinking in terms of beginnings and endings, this idea can be difficult to accept. We are a goal-driven people who find anything that has no clear-cut end game, so to speak, pointless, and therefore we often reject this option outright on that basis alone. As a result, most modern New Age purveyors suggest that we simply choose to end the cycle whenever we wish and remain within the spiritual realm—our need to come back into the flesh sated and our little adventure here on planet Earth effectively finished. In effect, we can choose to stop reincarnating.

What happens after that, however, is where the debate gets serious. Do we simply exist in some sort of eternal state of nirvana, or do we perhaps move on to other realms of existence—other dimensions, if you will—to experience things in an entirely different context?

We have no idea how vast the entire realm of existence may be, so the idea that there may be other venues by which the Divine might come to "know itself" that do not include insertion into the physical realm has to be considered. However, that is not the only option available to us. Another possibility suggested by some is that upon finishing our earthly adventure and effectively coming to complete enlightenment, we might choose to come into the flesh again, only this time it would not be to mature spiritually but to help other souls along their own path toward self-realization. In essence, once we have finished the process, we might come back into the flesh in service to others so they may also find enlightenment and thus finish their own journeys.

Certainly there is some logic to the idea of mature souls returning to the flesh in service for others. There are many who consider Buddha to have been an enlightened soul who did precisely that, while others imagine Jesus, Gandhi, Krishna, the Dalai Lama, and a host of other spiritual leaders to be manifestations of enlightened souls—known as "avatars"—who came from the realm of spirit to bring enlightenment to an entire world. It would be a difficult path to be sure, as humanity has a nasty tendency to stone its own prophets, but a necessary one if we are to grow collectively as a people. It wouldn't be something for every soul to attempt, but I suspect there are many who would be tempted to try it, and many who have in the past even if the outcomes of those attempts have been lost to history. Undoubtedly, history has hosted a pantheon of failed avatars, most of whom will never be known, and will continue to do so until humanity ultimately finds its way and finally negates the need for more guides to lead us to the light.

And, finally, there is one other possibility to consider: once our soul is absorbed back into the greater realm of spirit—perhaps to join all the other souls who have also finished their adventure—we might simply and collectively choose to separate into an infinite number of "God pieces" once more and start the entire process over again. In effect, once the game is finished, we may collectively choose to start a new game, though this time with new goals and entirely reworked agendas in mind. It may be that we will always have an infinite number of possibilities placed before us and an eternity to explore each in turn, making this adventure we call life an ongoing and never-ending one that will consume every moment of existence forever. Such would be like the beating of a divine heart, with each beat creating an entirely new reality to be realized and a new set of infinite possibilities to be explored.

Clearly, it appears that just as in life, the prospects of what happens "next" from a spiritual perspective are equally as vast. Of course, I realize how difficult it may be to grasp such a prospect on an intellectual basis, so perhaps the following parable might help. At a minimum, it should be sufficient to elicit some thought about where the process ultimately takes us and what we might do with what we've learned when we finish. I call it the parable of the student and the Master.

––––––

Once there was a young man who dreamed of painting like one of the great Masters. It was all he thought of day and night and, after years of admiring their work and studying their techniques, one day he decided to attempt to be a great painter himself. Though nervous and unsure of himself, he obtained all the necessary supplies he would require, sat down to his canvas, and went to work.

He labored for months on his piece, sketching out the various elements, drawing and redrawing as necessary, painting and even reworking entire sections until finally, after great effort, he felt he was finished. He was happily admiring his work when, to his great surprise, one of the very Masters he was attempting to emulate entered the room carrying a canvas of his own under one arm. Without a word, he sat his painting on an easel next to the young artist's and quietly took a seat next to him.

The young man was crestfallen by what he saw. He had imagined his painting to be on par with those of the greatest artists of the age, but now that he could compare the works side by side he could see how amateurish and inept his painting was. Distraught, he poured out to the Master how badly he had failed, how his sense of perspective was askew, how the composition was sadly lacking, how his use of color was entirely inadequate. The great Master simply smiled and patiently waited for the young man to finish his damning self-critique.

"Do you wish to try again?" he asked gently.

The young man blinked back tears and stared at the old man. "I don't know," he answered uncertainly. "I want nothing more than to be a great painter myself, but I don't seem to have it in me. I've failed."

"No," the Master gently chided. "You haven't failed. You simply have not achieved your goal yet. A great painter already lives within you, waiting to emerge. You simply need to let him out. Try again."

With that the Master went on to point out to the young man his successes and review the things he had learned even through his failed attempt. With encouragement in his wise old eyes, the Master offered him a fresh canvas and told him to start anew.

"Only do not paint the same picture," he instructed him patiently. "Try a completely new scene, a different landscape, another palette. Do not forget the lessons you have learned, but apply them to this new work."

Encouraged, the young man eagerly set about producing a second painting, enthusiastically applying what he had learned from his earlier piece. After many months and several false starts, he finally managed to produce a second work that even he could see was clearly far superior to the first, and excitement filled his heart.

Just as he was busy admiring his newest creation, however, the Master walked in with his own freshly painted canvas once again, this one carrying a scene reminiscent of the one the young artist had painted, and placed it on an easel next to that of the young novice's for comparison. Though the student could see that his own new painting was better than his previous work, he could easily see that it was still far from matching the Master's skills and so, once more, the young man was discouraged.

As before, however, the Master did not permit him to dwell on his disappointment. Just as he had done earlier, he patiently pointed out the new painting's flaws and its mistakes, but he also pointed out how it was a dramatic improvement over the student's earlier effort. The Master encouraged the student to try again, and the student agreed— not only because of the Master's unwavering faith and encouragement, but also because he recognized he had indeed improved and believed he could do better if he tried yet again.

So for a third time the novice, who by now had been striving toward his goal for many years, started a new painting. Again, after several false starts, he finally produced another work: this one his finest to date. No sooner had he had applied the final brushstroke, however, when, like clockwork, the Master appeared with his own similar piece for a comparison. This time, however, the young man was not so discouraged. He could see it was still not up to the level of the Master's work, but he could also see—as the Master pointed out himself—that he was getting closer.

A fourth, fifth, and sixth canvas followed, and each time the young man refined his work until it began to mimic that of the Great Master himself. One day, after many years of laboring on his greatest piece, the Master appeared one more time to examine the work, placing his own painting alongside the new piece. This time, however, the two pieces were—though not identical—equally perfect. Neither the student nor his teacher could find anything that required refinement.

"You have no need to paint any longer, my student," the Master said quietly. "You are now a Master yourself."

The aspiring painter at first wept tears of joy at the fact he had at last achieved his goal but then he stopped abruptly as the Master's words found their way into his consciousness. "I have no need to paint anymore?" he asked, confused. "But why? Now that I can paint like one of the great Masters, why should I stop?"

"Because there is nothing more you can learn. You have achieved mastery, and there is no further road to travel. Anything you paint from now on will simply be redundant."

"But what then shall I do?" he asked. "I have worked all my life for this moment. What else can I do?"

"Indeed," the Master replied. "What else *can* you do? Once you reach mastery, there are many paths open, many roads that you may travel. You can stop painting and simply rest in the knowledge that you have achieved the mastery you have always sought, of course, or you can continue to paint masterpieces until you have filled the world with beauty. You can also choose a most difficult road and decide to show others how to paint as a Master, despite the hardship and pain that may entail. And, finally, you may choose to start the process over again. Forget all you have learned about becoming a great painter and start from the beginning, moving over that same ground again—only experiencing the process of learning to become a great Master in a different way."

The Master drew closer. "You may even wish to move down another path entirely and, having mastered painting, learn to be a great writer, musician, or sculptor instead. As I said, there are many paths and as always, the possibilities are inexhaustible."

"But which is the nobler path?" the student-turned-Master asked.

"Each path is equally noble. They are all useful and each carries its own rewards and consequences. There is no possibility that one might choose incorrectly, for all paths lead to mastery of something."

"Do I have to decide now?"

The Master shook his head and smiled. "No, my child. You have all eternity in which to decide, and an eternity to decide not to decide, if that is your desire. But know that which path you choose will be the one that's right for you, for all paths are the right ones, for they are all ordained of God."

With that the old Master rose to his feet, took his painting, and quietly shuffled out of the room, leaving his former student to ponder his destiny. He left in joy, however, pleased that now the new Master understood.

———

That's how it is with reincarnation. Each incarnation is a fresh canvas upon which we place the brushstrokes of life. Sometimes we choose to begin again with a new canvas. Sometimes our canvas is destroyed before we've had a chance to complete it, though usually we manage to finish the piece, and when we die—or leave this current incarnation—we have the opportunity to appraise our work and judge what we have placed upon the canvas. Quickly we see where we have "failed" and, conversely, where we have succeeded, by judging our own piece against the perfect canvas we call God. Eventually, once we are ready to try again, we receive a fresh canvas and begin once again. The old painting is forgotten and buried; in fact, so intent are we on painting this new picture that we scarcely recall the old one at all. Even so, the lessons it provided remain within us to become an element of this new canvas until finally, one day, our personal masterpiece is finished. That is when we decide whether we wish to stop painting and break the wheel of multiple rebirths, to go on painting through numerous reincarnations—painting vastly different landscapes on each new canvas—or whether we will choose to teach others. Or we may even choose to start the whole thing over again and enjoy the process throughout eternity. The choice is ours, just as it has been from the beginning and just as it always will remain.

Conclusion

One common objection to the concept of reincarnation is that the very act of contemplating what might have happened to us in a past life only serves to clutter our present life with unnecessary distractions, thereby preventing us, it is thought, from living life in the here and now. While I agree we need to live in the present (which is, after all, the only thing that genuinely exists within our current frame of reference), considering reincarnation, or pondering any area of the survivability of the soul for that matter, does not seem to me to take away from the fine art of living. In fact, I have found quite the opposite to be the case.

I personally find reincarnation to be far more than an ancient Eastern postmortem hypothesis. Reincarnation is what allows us to see our existence not in the context of a single brief earthly visit but rather in the context of a hundred such visits. It gives the past and the future meaning and in so doing gives the present purpose, for it is only in fusing all three elements of existence—past, present, and future—that life begins to make sense. It allows us the luxury of recognizing that our death is not the end of life but only the beginning of another, and permits us to live out our life without self-recrimination, knowing that everything we've done—no matter how selfish or petty or mean spirited—is a part of the sometimes painful process of spiritual maturation. It also permits us the dignity of securing our own salvation, not through some carte-blanche absolution resulting from membership in a particular religion or allegiance to a specific creed, but by taking responsibility for our own lives and actions and learning to grow beyond our very human frailties and weaknesses.

Reincarnation also gives us the gift of accepting that we don't need to realize every hope and dream in the context of this single brief lifetime, for the opportunities we wish we'd had in this life may be realized in the next lifetime, or in the one after that, or the one after that. Consider how many people might find comfort in this life knowing that those things they've always wanted to do but lacked the time, resources, energy, or courage to try may yet be realized in a future incarnation—that the unrealized dreams of being a great musician, an acclaimed actor, a gifted leader, a daring explorer, or even of simply bearing the children a barren womb has robbed them of, are not out of reach but merely on hold. Or how much joy might the knowledge that those things we once loved doing but can no longer do now because of age, sickness, or distance can be realized once again, albeit in another time and place. Reincarnation is the mechanism through which we may live the very life we've always wanted—or relive the one we've always loved—upon a stage from which we may act out a million possibilities, dream a billion dreams, and live on throughout eternity. If that fails to appeal to the deepest longings of the human heart, then I can't imagine what might do it.

That reincarnation is true must remain an element of faith (just as does the belief that it isn't true), but if we deny its reality, what is left of this thing we call life? As for myself, I can only say that the idea that this life is all there is and that our consciousness does not survive death is like imagining that love does not exist but is only a silly notion we have invented to keep ourselves from feeling lonely and unappreciated. Yet we know that love is real, for we have all felt it. It is as real as the affection we feel for our spouse and the tears we shed the first time we hold our newborn child, and so I choose to believe that love and life, like the universe we live in, are eternal as well.

And while reincarnation is the way I see eternity being played out on the human stage, we would be wise to remember that it is only one small part of the equation and not even the most important part. Yet it was in embracing the concept that the enormity of the universe and the untapped potential of the human spirit was realized for me, for it demonstrated to me that we live through multiple incarnations, and in that I found a rhyme and reason to the cosmos that I never knew existed before.

Truly, we are on a quest—a quest for knowledge and understanding, but most of all a quest to know the Divine in ways we could never appreciate otherwise. That is the gift reincarnation gives us. It is the gift of God.

Bibliography

Banerjee, H. N. *Americans Who Have Been Reincarnated*. New York: Macmillan, 1980.

Bernstein, Morey. *The Search for Bridey Murphy*. New York: Doubleday, 1956.

Cranston, Sylvia, and Carey Williams. *Reincarnation: A New Horizon in Science, Religion, and Society*. New York: Julian Press, 1984.

Fiore, Edith. *You Have Been Here Before*. New York: Ballantine, 1978.

Goldberg, Bruce. *Past Lives, Future Lives*. New York: Ballantine, 1982.

Lenz, Frederick. *Lifetimes: True Accounts of Reincarnation*. New York: Ballantine, 1979.

MacGregor, Geddes. *Reincarnation as a Christian Hope*. Totowa, NJ: Barnes & Noble, 1982.

———. *Reincarnation in Christianity: A New Vision of the Role of Rebirth in Christian Thought*. Wheaton, IL: Theosophical Publishing House, 1978.

Moody, Raymond. *Coming Back: A Psychiatrist Explores Past-Life Journeys*. New York: Bantam, 1991.

Newton, Michael. *Destiny of Souls: New Case Studies of Life Between Lives*. St. Paul, MN: Llewellyn, 2000.

———. *Journey of Souls: Case Studies of Life Between Lives*. St. Paul, MN: Llewellyn, 1994.

———. *Life Between Lives: Hypnotherapy for Spiritual Regression*. St. Paul, MN: Llewellyn, 2004.

Newton, Michael, ed. *Memories of the Afterlife*. Woodbury, MN: Llewellyn, 2009.

Pagels, Elaine. *The Gnostic Gospels*. New York: Random House, 1979.

Shroder, Tom. *Old Souls: The Scientific Evidence for Past Lives*. New York: Simon & Schuster, 1999.

Snow, Robert L. *Looking for Carroll Beckwith: The True Story of a Detective's Search for His Past Life*. Emmaus, PA: Daybreak Books, 1999.

Stevenson, Ian. *Children Who Remember Previous Lives: A Question of Reincarnation*, revised edition. Jefferson, NC: McFarland, 2001.

———. *Twenty Cases Suggestive of Reincarnation*. Charlottesville, VA: University Press of Virginia, 1974.

Wambach, Helen. *Reliving Past Lives: The Evidence Under Hypnosis*. New York: Harper & Row, 1978.

Weiss, Brian. *Many Lives, Many Masters*. New York: Simon & Schuster, 1988.

Whitton, Joel L. *Life Between Life*. New York: Warner Books, 1986.

Wilson, Colin. *Beyond the Occult*. New York: Carroll & Graf, 1989.

Woolger, Roger. *Other Lives, Other Selves*. New York: Bantam, 1988.

To Write to the Author

If you wish to contact the author or would like more information about this book, please write to the author in care of Llewellyn Worldwide and we will forward your request. Both the author and publisher appreciate hearing from you and learning of your enjoyment of this book and how it has helped you. Llewellyn Worldwide cannot guarantee that every letter written to the author can be answered, but all will be forwarded. Please write to:

J. Allan Danelek
% Llewellyn Worldwide Ltd.
2143 Wooddale Drive
Woodbury, MN 55125-2989
Please enclose a self-addressed stamped envelope for reply,
or $1.00 to cover costs. If outside the USA, enclose
an international postal reply coupon.

Many of Llewellyn's authors have websites with additional information and resources. For more information, please visit our website at http://www.llewellyn.com.

The Case for Ghosts
An Objective Look at the Paranormal
J. Allan Danelek

What are ghosts? Can anyone become one after death? How do they interact with time and space? Stripping away the sensationalism and fraud linked to this contentious topic, J. Allan Danelek presents a well-researched study of a phenomenon that has fascinated humanity for centuries.

Analyzing both side of the issue by examining theories that support and debunk supernatural events, Danelek objectively explores hauntings, the ghost psyche, spirit communication, and spirit guides. He also investigates spirit photography, EVPs, ghost-hunting tools, Ouija boards, and the darker side of the ghost equation—malevolent spirits and demon possession. Whether you're a ghost enthusiast or a skeptic, *The Case for Ghosts* promises amazing insights into the spirit realm.

978-0-7387-0865-2, 240 pp., 6 x 9   **$12.95**

Atlantis: Lessons from the Lost Continent

J. ALLAN DANELEK

Is the Atlantis story a myth, pseudo-science, or a true story with lessons for our future? Objective and scrupulous, J. Allan Danelek applies his signature no-nonsense approach to the legend of the Lost Continent.

Investigating geosciences, traditional theories, Plato's dialogues, and historical maps, Danelek attempts to answer the questions surrounding this twelve-thousand-year-old legend. Did Atlantis truly exist? If so, what was its culture like? How did the Atlanteans destroy themselves? Why haven't we found any hard evidence of this civilization? And finally, what can we learn from the fate of Atlantis—an advanced civilization perhaps not unlike our own?

This engaging exploration of Atlantis brings clarity to a controversial subject and offers reasonable and fascinating theories of what may have happened to this ancient civilization.

978-0-7387-1162-1, 264 pp., 6 x 9   **$15.95**

To order, call 1-877-NEW-WRLD
Prices subject to change without notice
Order at Llewellyn.com 24 hours a day, 7 days a week!

UFOs: The Great Debate

*An Objective Look at Extraterrestrials, Government
Cover-Ups, and the Prospect of First Contact*

J. ALLAN DANELEK

Do UFOs really exist? Are we alone in the universe? Is the government hiding the truth from us? With his customary objective and balanced approach, J. Allan Danelek explores the controversial questions that have raged for years about extraterrestrials.

This wide-ranging and captivating book begins with a historical overview of the decades-long debate, followed by an incisive look at the case for and against extraterrestrial intelligence. Danelek presents scientific evidence supporting UFOs and other life-sustaining planets, examines hoaxes, and raises practical objections based on radar findings and satellite observations. Next, he delves into alleged government conspiracies and cover-ups—including Roswell, alien visitation, and alien technology. There's also intriguing speculation about the potential alien "agenda" and suggestions of possible scenarios, both benign and malevolent, for first contact with an alien species.

978-0-7387-1383-0, 264 pp., 6 x 9 $15.95

To order, call 1-877-NEW-WRLD
Prices subject to change without notice
Order at Llewellyn.com 24 hours a day, 7 days a week!

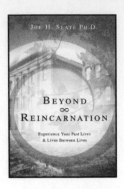

Beyond Reincarnation

Experience Your Past Lives & Lives Between Lives

JOE H. SLATE, PH.D.

Explore past lives, communicate with the departed, meet spirit guides. . . . According to Dr. Joe Slate, accessing the spirit realm is not only possible, it's beneficial for our present lives and future spiritual evolution. Past-life knowledge can offer direction and balance, explain fears and compulsions, build self-worth, and promote acceptance of others.

This introduction to reincarnation examines the mind/body/spirit connection and the existence of the ageless soul. Also presented here are Dr. Slate's simple, laboratory-tested strategies for exploring the nonphysical world. Readers can learn how to probe past lives and preexistence through self-hypnosis, astral travel to new spiritual dimensions, and communication with spirits through table tipping. The author's own fascinating experiences, along with personal accounts of his subjects who have tested his techniques, are also included.

978-0-7387-0714-3, 216 pp., 6 x 9 $14.95

Journey of Souls
Case Studies of Life Between Lives
MICHAEL NEWTON, PH.D.

This remarkable book uncovers the mystery of life in the spirit world after death on Earth. Dr. Michael Newton has developed his own hypnosis technique to reach his subjects' hidden memories of the hereafter. The narrative is woven as a progressive travel log around the accounts of twenty-nine people who were placed in a state of super-consciousness. While in deep hypnosis, these subjects describe what has happened to them between their former reincarnations on earth. They reveal graphic details about how it feels to die, who meets us right after death, what the spirit world is really like, where we go and what we do as souls, and why we choose to come back in certain bodies.

After reading *Journey of Souls*, you will acquire a better understanding of the immortality of the human soul. Plus, you will meet day-to-day personal challenges with a greater sense of purpose as you begin to understand the reasons behind events in your own life.

978-1-56718-485-3, 288 pp., 6 x 9 $16.95

Destiny of Souls
New Case Studies of Life Between Lives
MICHAEL NEWTON, PH.D.

A pioneer in uncovering the secrets of life, internationally recognized spiritual hypnotherapist Dr. Michael Newton takes you into the heart of the spirit world. His best-selling books are the definitive study on the afterlife. In *Destiny of Souls*, Dr. Newton presents seventy case histories of real people who were regressed into their lives between lives. Dr. Newton answers requests from the thousands of people who want more details about various aspects of life on the other side. *Destiny of Souls* is also designed for the enjoyment of first-time readers who haven't read his other books, such as *Journey of Souls*.

978-1-56718-499-0, 432 pp., 6 x 9   **$16.95**